CLUELESS

The story of two extraordinary financial mysteries, huge investor losses and a brilliantly straightforward blueprint for your future success...

BRIAN DENNEHY

COPYRIGHT

ISBN: 978-1-9998062-1-7

Edition: December 2017

Dedication

For my mum

Acknowledgements

Writing a book is daunting, but you really only discover this when you try. As a result, the authors of the books which have most influenced me over years are now multiples higher in my estimation.

I feel like I grew up with Kindleberger and his *Manias Panics and Crashes*. In more recent years James Montier has provided lucidity to behavioural finance, and his work is a "must read". James P. O'Shaughnessy regular updates his eye-opening tome, *What Works On Wall Street*. Daniel Kahneman, decades after his ground-breaking research in the 1970s, continues to educate us all. Peter L. Bernstein has produced a classic trilogy on investment, markets, and risk, sweeping majestically across centuries. Last but not least, Elroy Dimson and his colleagues at London Business School have been poking the investment industry with insightful research for a couple of decades. Thank you to all these extraordinary guys.

The Dennehy Weller & Co team, led by Linden Weller, have been essential in helping me create the time to persevere with this book.

My children, Tara and Ruairi, have given input from early drafts. You certainly get a different perspective from younger people!

My physiotherapist played her part, encouraging me to spend more time behind a desk, and less time doing daft outdoor activities.

Thank you to my marvelous clients and the thousands of people who have already invested just a little time in reading my earlier work. Many have given me new insights, and this book is to give them all something back.

Last but not least, thank you to my partner Fiona (an extraordinarily tidy person) who didn't blink as I spread mountains of books and papers around a large number of rooms, and worked manfully to keep my stress under control.

About Brian Dennehy

Brian Dennehy's extensive experience as an investment adviser stretches back to 1987, when he was a co-founder of independent financial advisers and chartered financial planners **Dennehy Weller & Co.** He also founded **FundExpert.co.uk**, and has been the main contributor to the acclaimed ***TopFunds Guide*** since its launch in 2002.

With more than thirty years' experience in the investment and financial services industry, he is passionate about achieving the best possible outcomes for clients through ground-breaking research.

His long-term commitment to uncovering outstanding investment solutions is evidenced by his media coverage week after week for more than 20 years - in The Times, Telegraph, Financial Times, What Investment and Mail on Sunday among others. Plus TV and radio appearances including BBC and Sky.

Brian's idea of fun is taking part in challenges such as the grueling Marathon de Sables, ice-climbing in the Scottish mountains, with the odd triathlon thrown in for good measure! However, encouraged by his physiotherapist, he thought it was time to write a book and give something back to both the clients and the industry who have treated him well.

Brian is a law graduate, Fellow of the Personal Finance Society, and a Chartered Financial Planner.

Contents

INTRODUCTION

VAST SUMS HAD gone missing.

Something needed to be done.

If this was my quiet instinct in the late 1980s, it came into very sharp focus over the next two decades as the evidence grew and grew...

And so did the sums which were missing.

There was a lot of detective work to do. It took me years of effort to get to the bottom of this mystery, uncovering clues as to what had gone on. And, more importantly for me, I wanted to protect my clients.

It is the story of those years I am now sharing with you - plus a highly practical blueprint for your investing success.

Who was the victim? There were many. At least one victim lost £808,446 – most lost more. No one seemed to care. This was curious because such losses were not isolated. In fact, these losses were viral. On one of my calculations, the total sums languishing amount to £35 billion.[1]

Yet the victims had no name. They remained anonymous. **And there was no outcry**.

It was bizarre. **Could losses which were so large and so widespread just happen by accident?** Was it just "one of those things"?

If it wasn't an accident, it must have been deliberate. If deliberate, it feels like robbery. But no one noticed. This was robbery by stealth.

Who knew? A good number of people knew. Fund groups, and the better advisers and more experienced journalists. But they either misunderstood the nature of this mystery, or they had other priorities, so they did little or nothing about it.

The authorities, the government, and the regulators should have known, and acted. They haven't (at least not so far). The media have skirted around the issue occasionally, but mostly missed the clues.

Yet the clues to solving this mystery are not just all around us today – as I will show you. But they were laid down years ago, even decades ago.

The story has heroes and villains: there is the tale of two Harry's; a man who stopped Napoleon in his tracks; an accidental meeting which changed the world; piratical fund managers; big brains and little common sense; and more than one pivotal person who just needed to get out more!

What happened? Over decades, the evidence piled up that the investing public was, at a minimum, being badly served. This evidence was so pervasive that it makes "badly served" sound like horrible understatement. Our research showed that 92% of funds bought by the public were mediocre at best[2], but this news was far from new – similar concerns were raised as far back as the 1960s.

To understand what happened requires some detective work which begins even further back, in 1774, and continues to this day.

I am going to take you on a journey to understand this mystery – because that is the antidote to *you* avoiding viral losses.

By the end of this book I will provide you with a highly practical blueprint to put you on the road to success, and which you can enjoy for many years to come. If you use it consistently, this blueprint can genuinely transform your life.

As you read this book, and go on this journey with me, it will become increasingly clear to you that you now have a formula for success – you don't need to belong to the multitude of victims.

In the first chapter I will give you a glimpse of what success looks like – as I said, it can be genuinely life-changing.

PART I

Want to get a head start? No problem.
Go to *FundExpert.co.uk/quickstart*

I am determined to help you transform your investing success. You don't need to take daft risks; you don't need special skills; you don't need more time.

You just need a clear and proven process to select outstanding funds, and the discipline to apply it. **Process and discipline.**

We will not just provide the process, but also use our smart technology to keep you on the straight and narrow, and alert you if there are problems. **Plus**:

- **Your own "Winning Funds Blueprint"**. Typically the building block of a report which would cost £500 as a minimum.
- **Worked examples** to guide your next steps.
- **Your burning questions?** I will answer them in my live teleconference.
- **Top-performing model portfolios**, including performance updates.
- **LATEST** winning funds report, sector by sector, to finish your blueprint.
- The latest edition of the acclaimed **TopFunds Guide**, usual cost £50.
- **Our historical research.**

How would you feel if all of this was free?
That would be bonkers wouldn't it?

Go to *FundExpert.co.uk/quickstart*

1. Bad News for Them, GREAT News for You

In this chapter, I want to give you a sense of the scale of the problem, a glimpse of what success looks like (and it is impressive), and deal with some housekeeping issues. But we must never lose sight of one fact.

Investing in funds is a great idea. From their humble beginnings, investment funds have given all of us the opportunity to participate in the dynamism and profitability of not just our own economy, but exciting opportunities around the globe.

Yet there is a culture of complacency. Too many fund investors accept mediocrity (at best) when, by making better choices, they can transform their financial well-being and their lives – that is not an exaggeration, as I will show you.

When investing your money, you are confronted with three problems, whether you are a millionaire or a novice, whether building a portfolio or growing your SIPP, or simply making an ISA contribution:

- The great majority of funds are not good enough.
- Most people find it extremely difficult to recognise funds with outstanding potential.
- And the timing of investors is shockingly bad.

The difference between successful investing and mediocrity is stark – this is the case whether you invest in funds or individual shares. Although the story told in this book will enable you to transform your investing in funds, much of what you will learn applies equally to shares.

Even for the most ardent investor in shares, funds should be playing a part in your portfolio, whether to access the huge potential of overseas markets or a highly specialised area such as high yield bonds.

For many others, funds dominate their portfolio, ISAs, SIPPs and pension plans. If you can consistently select funds with the greatest potential, the results can extraordinary, as I will illustrate.

But the problem at the heart of this book is that the great majority of funds are mediocre at best.

Here is the raw statistic:

92% of funds are mediocre at best[2]

92%

If you are investing into these funds (and the odds are that you are), it is costing you a lot of money.

But it is not all bad news. This is also GREAT news, because it makes it easier to spot the small number of outstanding funds, and I am going to help you do just that.

It is also good news because the scale of failure provides plenty of raw material for us to explore as we try and understand why so many clever people appear to get it so consistently *wrong*. This will make it easier to identify the ingredients you need to be consistently *right:* i.e. what it takes for you to be consistently successful.

I know some of you will get a sinking feeling at this stage.

"How can I possibly do better than those clever City types?"

You really don't need to have an inferiority complex. I will show you why in some detail. For now, you just need to keep in mind that you can do things which they can't. And that only one person is really motivated to make the most of your money – you.

Let me get two other issues out of the way.

Firstly, what you are going to learn **does not involve you taking unusual or extreme risks**. If you already own funds, it simply means making better decisions – obviously lots to come on that.

Secondly, **it doesn't require special expertise**. In fact, you can take the steps I will show you even if you are a relative novice, perhaps taking your first steps to invest in an ISA or SIPP.

Let's give this some context and see what success looks like.

Here's how you could have done if you had a process to select funds with outstanding potential **and** applied it with discipline over an extended period, in this case from 1994 to 2014. This is a long enough period to take in a number of bumps in the road – the Asian financial crisis, the tech bubble, the Great Financial Crisis of 2007-8.

This is what success looks like, if you invested £100,000 in 1994:[3]

> £100,000 grew to **£1,197,100** using a proven, simple process to select funds.

Alternatively...

> £100,000 became **£392,050** if you invested into an index tracking fund.

That's a HUGE difference between those two numbers – between success and mediocrity.

I will explore this example in more detail later. For now, this is a great example of how good it can be for you, *providing that you have a clear plan and stick with it.*

You do not need to take daft risks. You just need to buy ordinary funds but VERY selectively, using a process which is both simple and repeatable year after year.

This book is designed to help you begin to build your plan around such a process. But I also make it easy to "stick with it", as you will see later – I am not going to abandon you once you put this book down, I promise.

This is the order of play:

So far, we have touched on the elements of the mystery, and quantified the scale of losses. I have also given you a glimpse of the huge benefits to you if you can turn this around.

From chapters 3-11, I will explore how we got to where we are today. This is all brought together in chapter 12.

In the second half of the book (from chapter 13), I develop a solution which will work for you, with a volume of evidence showing what your success will look like.

In chapter 24 is **your blueprint for success, which you can start today** – to ensure you are not another victim of complacency and mediocrity.

Last but not least, chapter 25. Here is the key which unlocks the ultimate value of the blueprint.

But right now, I would prefer if you didn't jump the gun – we have a journey to take together.

CLUES

- 92% of funds cannot beat a basic performance target most of the time.
- The good news is that this narrows down the outstanding funds.
- You need to be able to identify outstanding funds today that are highly likely to be outstanding funds tomorrow...
- ...and have a way to identify when such funds run out of steam and need replacing.
- I don't believe the solution requires special skills or experience on your part...
- ...nor does the solution involve you taking any additional risks, as I will show you later.

NEXT STEPS

I want to show you how one simple, effective, method to select funds can transform your success – and how this is *your* choice.

2. How This Hurts You — The Evidence

There are enough outstanding funds, that is clear to me. The problem is that most of your money is almost certainly not invested into these funds.

Do you realise how poor most funds are?

We know this at FundExpert because we crunched the numbers – in huge detail over many years, and in various ways, so as not to miss an angle.

In one piece of research, our objective was simply to identify funds with consistent longer-term performance – in particular, above average performance most of the time in the prior 10 years.

Our test was simple:

> **An outstanding fund is one which is in the top 40% of performers for 60% of the time.**

We didn't think this was hugely challenging but, when we did our original research in 2014, 92% of funds failed to beat this simple benchmark.

We were surprised.

By our definition, this meant that 92% were mediocre at best. (This number changed little in subsequent updates)

This research became the basis for our *Vintage Ratings*[4]. The detailed results of this particular research are beyond the scope of this book; nonetheless it is very informative to highlight the key findings.

We split all funds into Vintage, Mediocre, or Ugly. A Vintage fund was one that met our test.

We discovered that the Vintage-rated funds grew more than twice as much as the *Ugly* funds at the bottom of the pile. Those *Ugly* funds represented a huge **£35 billion** of investor money. A differential this great results in extraordinarily polarised outcomes for people with the same objective.

For example, imagine that you are 20 years before retirement and your objective is to grow your pension fund primarily through investing into UK stock market funds – the main sector containing these funds is called *UK All Companies*.

Vintage-rated funds in this sector enjoyed **152%** growth, on average, over the 10 years to June 2016. That's a growth rate of 9.7% per annum.

In contrast the average Ugly-rated fund in the same sector grew by just **62%**, or 5% per annum.

If this repeated itself over the next 20 years, there are two versions of your retirements:

> **Version 1. A comfortable retirement**, and you might even retire early.
>
> **Why?** Because you got it right, you had a successful proven process to select funds.
>
> OR
>
> **Version 2. Scrape along in retirement**, and possibly have to work much longer than intended.
>
> **Why?** Because you never addressed the key issue – how to select funds with outstanding potential.

With version 2, where you never got to grips with how to select funds, your pension fund is 35% lower than version 1, where you applied a proven process to select funds.

Imagine you were told today that your income tomorrow would be 35% lower – not just tomorrow, but permanently.

How would you feel?

Shocked?

Annoyed?

Looking for someone to blame?

That is the risk you take unless you pay attention to this problem and the clues we uncover in our unfolding story.

It gets worse, because the consequences of this persist, perhaps for another 30 years in retirement.

Your outcome could be even more extreme than this. The above numbers are based on averages. The actual results for many people will be much worse. And for a smaller number of people, the results will be much better, and I will show you how they will do it.

If this glimpse into a possible future of yours makes you feel uncomfortable or even angry, then remind yourself that it is within your control *now* to do something about it.

I'm here to make sure you do **not** make these mistakes. I will show you simple things that you can do which fund managers cannot do. And these "things" mean that you can even generate better performance than some of the world's best-known fund managers, including the likes of Neil Woodford and Warren Buffett.

That's a crazy thought isn't it. But I will show you the evidence for what appears to be an outrageous statement.

This does not involve you in taking daft risks.

It just means making better decisions.

And probably involving you in a lot less effort (and stress).

In this chapter, I simply wanted to illustrate that you have choices, and that your choice will have a heavy impact on the future quality of your life.

You can allow yourself to stumble into poor funds, or you can take charge.

I have illustrated my point here using our ***Vintage Ratings*, and they are impressive**. But in the rest of this book, I will reveal another method, what I will prove is by far the most successful process for selecting funds.

Once you have been on this journey with me, **you will have a vastly better chance of achieving success with a new depth of knowledge**.

Think of this depth of knowledge as the foundation on which your success will be built, giving you the confidence to apply what you have learnt – **and stick with it!**

Clues

- Getting your fund selection wrong can decimate your life plans...
- ...getting it right can transform them.
- The differences between the best and worst are very extreme.
- **You can choose** between these outcomes – it is not out of your control.

NEXT STEPS

Now I'm going to take you back in time, to uncover clues as to how we got to where we are today, for better and worse.

3. Once Upon a Time

There are two old sayings which sit hand-in-glove:

- You must speculate to accumulate.
- Don't have all your eggs in one basket.

Together they are the pillars of your success; apart they are at the heart of regular and sometimes spectacular failure.

The late 18th century was a time of great colonial adventures by the British and Dutch, with huge fortunes to be made. But there were also risks, and failure was expensive. So, it was a good time to consider pooling the resources of lots of people across a number of ventures, so they could both enjoy the rewards and not have all of their eggs in one basket.

Against this backdrop, a Dutch merchant, Adriaan Van Ketwich, had the foresight to pool money from a number of people to create a fund – the world's first fund – in 1774. The fund spread financial risk by having interests across a number of European countries and the American colonies – in other words, the fund was diversified.

What might surprise us is that at this early stage there was a very formal structure requiring diversification within the fund. It had to be invested across 20 "classes", and each class spread across 50 bonds, and the fund should "observe as much as possible an equal proportionately".

Why such an explicit and formal requirement for diversification? This seems quite sophisticated for the very first fund.

The reason is very familiar to us today – the banks had got themselves into a pickle and this severely dampened risk appetite. In 1772-1773, British banks were bankrupted (yes, this is not new!) by having too great an exposure to the British East India Company.

So, this explicit diversification was a marketing wheeze! Similar funds launched just afterwards specifically advertised the benefits of diversification to attract small investors.

The opening paragraph of one included this line.[5]

> *"No one has reason to expect that all securities... will cease to pay off at the same time, and the entire capital be lost. If one had reason to fear such general bankruptcy, one never ought to invest any money."*

Quite. This goes to the heart of why funds are not just a good idea but a great idea.

As if to further hammer home the message, the name of the fund from whose prospectus this extract is taken is *Voordeelig and Voorsigtig* – "Profitable and Prudent". The first fund pioneers really understood the importance of the marketing message.

Nonetheless, it wasn't plain sailing for the first Van Ketwich fund, and others which followed close on its heels.

The success of these early funds was closely linked to the fortunes of plantation loans in the West Indies. A war between the Dutch and British and the American Revolution weren't helpful. By 1811, the Van Ketwich fund reached a low of 25% of its launch price. Nonetheless, it did recover and, in 1824, it was redeemed with a profit for investors, in addition to the dividends which had been paid out over the years.

Even with very explicit diversification, the journey for this fund was very rocky, though ultimately successful.

Most importantly, Van Ketwich's vehicle laid a foundation for the huge global industry we see today.

The fund idea spread from the Netherlands to England and France before heading to the U.S. in the 1890s.

The first fund (an investment trust in this case) outside the Netherlands was the Foreign & Colonial Government Trust, founded in 1868 in London. According to the prospectus, the goal was to provide:

> *"the investor of moderate means the same advantages as the large capitalist... by spreading the investment over a number of different stocks".*

As with the Van Ketwich fund, diversification – not having all of your eggs in one basket – was a fundamental attraction of funds.

The 1880s was a boom period for investment trusts in the UK. Though some failed during the British Crash of 1890 (when a banking crisis and too much debt would have taken the world into a depression but for a Government rescue – sound familiar?), most of them survived.

The first fund with a unit trust style was created in the U.S. in 1924, and these new types of funds performed (relatively) well in the Wall Street Crash of 1929. Soon after, in 1931, unit trusts arrived in Britain as a gift from the U.S. following a visit by a London stock broker. It was a brave plan being just after the Wall Street Crash and with the world in the grip of the Great Depression.[6]

Municipal & General Securities (todays M&G) launched the First British Fixed Trust on 22nd April 1931. It worked better than expected and soon had imitators. By 1939, there were 15 groups managing 89 trusts with a total value of £80 million.

By the end of the Second World War, the fund business was still a cottage industry, and the stock market was dominated by individual investors buying direct shareholdings. Buy-and-hold was the rule. Similarly, such institutional investors as existed seldom altered their portfolios, in an environment of negligible competition. "Rationalised laziness" observed one commentator. Later we will see if this is still a problem.

In the aftermath of the Second World War, restrictions were placed on new funds in the UK – in an austere post-war world it was not felt there was scope for surplus savings to go into funds.

> *"The orthodox opinion at the end of 1957 was that unit trusts were dead".*[7]

As is so often the case, orthodox opinion was totally wrong at the moment of greatest opportunity.

Investment trusts vs unit trusts - active funds vs passive funds

For the purposes of this book we do not need to get bogged down in the different technical structures between investment trusts, unit trusts and OEICS. The point is that the vast majority of such funds are actively managed - that is there is a fund manager in place actively thinking about the best ways to invest the assets of the fund. In contrast there are so-called passive funds or index trackers. In this case the typical funds automatically invest into the constituents of an index (e.g. the 100 companies which make up the FTSE 100 index) or a sector - the important point being that there is no fund manager input. These passive funds might be in the form of unit trusts or OEICS or, increasingly, within ETFs (exchange traded funds).

To reiterate, the most important differential in this book is that between actively managed funds and passive funds/index trackers.

The "cult of equities" began in 1958, and it wasn't long before Harold McMillan famously declared that most people in the UK "had never had it so good".

There was disillusionment around bonds and deposit accounts, and people who had never dreamt of buying stock market investments now wanted a slice of the action, and to share in the growing "*equity cult*".

The 1960s were a golden age for fund managers – known as "gunslingers" in the U.S. In the UK, it was said there was a "touch of the Spanish Main" about the funds and their managers. Yes, fund managers were likened to cowboys and pirates! But investors didn't seem to care. Few people seemed interested in precisely how their money was invested, though they should have been.

Unlike the 1950s, younger and more aggressive managers were being drawn to the glamour of the industry, and most fund groups were infected by the desire for "maximum performance". Among other emerging problems, the importance of a good spread of underlying shareholdings was being overlooked – in these over-confident times, diversification suddenly seemed less important.

There were hints that not all was well. As far back as 1933, Alfred Cowles conducted the most comprehensive research to date on forecasting services and concluded that investors could have done better with random selections picked out of a hat. Michael Jensen went further in 1969, covering 115 U.S. funds in the 10 years to 1964. He concluded that, on average, fund managers seemed unable to beat the markets with any convincing degree of consistency.

Nonetheless, it appeared difficult to go wrong with funds for UK investors.

Between 1956 and 1971, the average fund in the UK went up by 277%, compared with a 77% rise in the cost of living. By 1972, there was £2,647m invested in funds.

But markets were about to go into a tailspin, and gloom and despondency was to take hold.

The first significant generation of virgin fund investors were about to be taught a salutary lesson – markets do not keep going up in a straight line.

These were dark days from 1972-74, as markets fell 71%.[8]

Other important developments were taking place at this time. A new type of fund was on the near horizon. In the U.S. in 1971, Wells Fargo Bank launched the first index tracker, a fund mirroring a stock market index, with no active manager input – though such funds took a while to catch on.

From 1974, a stock market recovery began and fund sales leapt again – memories were short – another persistent failing of investors through the ages.

By 1983, just 9 years after the nadir of 1974, UK-based unit trusts were worth almost £12 billion.

The key was favourable demographics, the economy being lubricated by greater availability of debt, and the more favourable tax and regulatory treatment of unit trusts – which meant more funds, bigger fund groups, and expanding marketing budgets to take the message of funds to a much larger audience.

In parallel, after the pain of 1972-4 and in contrast to the gung-ho 1960s, much more attention was now being paid to the consistency of performance. Statistics and comparisons were more easily available, and there was a rapid increase in advisory services.

In the 1980s, there was something of a fund mania in actively managed funds, which built to a crescendo in 1987 – and then Crash on Black Monday, 19th October, when the U.S. stock market fell 22% in just one day. *[We have produced a history of this period. For a complimentary copy, go to FundExpert.co.uk/1987crash]*

After a breather, momentum built again in the 1990s. This was the Golden Age for unit trusts. Newspaper adverts for new funds proliferated, clipped coupons for applications flooded the offices of fund groups, and a new breed of no frills/no advice discount brokers flourished. After all, who needed advice – it was easy to make money!

With such over-confidence, it wasn't long before a serious mania took hold, and the craze for technology shares (and tech funds) led to the greatest stock market bubble of all time.

Institutional Complacency? Or Ignorance

If there was widespread complacency, if not also some ignorance, it was not confined to the novice investing coupon-clippers.

I recall one evening in 1999 when the UK government was announcing the launch of lower cost "Stakeholder Pensions". A member of the Government and a representative of the regulators appeared on Channel 4 news to announce that Stakeholder Pensions would emphasise "low cost and low risk index trackers". Oh dear. Index trackers? Low risk?

Index trackers are also called "passive" funds, but there is nothing passive about them. These are quite aggressive bets on the stock market, which is fine in the right hands. However, when the rationale for buying index trackers is primarily the low charges, investors are losing sight of the risks, and this typically happens in scale towards the end of a long upward run in the market. Put another way, "passive" investors lose sight of the risks just at the time they should be paying more attention e.g. 1999. How about 2017/8? We will see.

Anyway, back to 1999.

Despite the UK stock market falling 52%[9] from December 1999 to March 2003, and the big-selling technology funds losing 90%, the UK fund industry dusted itself off and boomed again from 2003 through the "noughties".

This new boom and enthusiasm for actively managed funds continued despite a persistent stream of research from the 1980s highlighting that the performance of most actively managed funds was simply not good enough. Vast sums were already going missing in this period.

The idea of funds started as a great innovation in the late 18th century to allow ordinary people to participate in great adventures, and to spread risk. But now, in modern times, something was wrong, not isolated but widespread. The mystery of how this happened cannot be solved until we discover:

- Why the industry grew despite such limited performance.
- Why the fund managers persistently struggle.

CLUES

That was quite a sweep across four centuries. What clues were there as to the nature of our mystery (i.e. huge investor losses), and ways in which we might not just sidestep such problems, but also achieve consistent investing success?

Quite a few, though it is too early in our journey to judge which are most relevant, and which are just a distraction:

- Diversification was a priority for the early funds.
- Markets have been prone to over-confidence, cults, bubbles, and manias.
- The latter periods are always followed by Crashes and ugly bear markets.

- These periods of over-confidence followed by panic appear with regularity.
- Research has frequently highlighted that most active funds are not good enough.
- The latter research has not stopped the huge expansion of the fund industry.
- Investor memories are short.
- Index tracking funds were introduced (partly) as a solution to poor active funds.

NEXT STEPS

It's now time to step back in time again to understand the historic research which influenced today's fund industry. This part of the story begins in Germany with Napoleon at the gates, and then jumps forward to a geeky student in post-Second World War Chicago.

4. Big Brains, No Common

Maths isn't everyone's cup of tea. In my experience, even people who excel at maths are inclined to get sucked into investments for a variety of poor reasons (glossy brochures, fund manager worship, or a great marketing story).

Yet if a mathematical formula could tell me how likely I am to make money, not lose money, and give me an idea of my profits and a timescale, I would be very interested.

That's probability.

Gottingen, Germany. 1807.

As bizarre as it might sound, mathematician Carl Freidrich Gauss was a world-class celebrity who worked on just that idea of probability (though not in a stock market context). His fame was such that, in 1807, as the French army approached his home town, Napoleon ordered his troops to spare Gottingen because "the greatest mathematician of all times is living there".

To mere mortals like myself, even his doctoral thesis title was impressive – "A New Proof That Every Rational Integer Function Of One Variable Can Be Resolved into Real Factors of the First or Second Degree". Phew.

For the avoidance of doubt, "like many mathematicians before and after him, Gauss was a childhood genius"[10].

Genius or not, he took a dim view of humanity and, literally, didn't get out much. Apparently in the last 27 years of his life, he only had one night away from home, and was most happy staying in and calculating the motion of heavenly bodies. He saw a "magical charm" in such matters.

Most significantly for the much later investment industry, he found a way to show a jumble of statistics in an orderly and meaningful way – the bell curve which came to play a key role in investment analysis.

In effect, the questions he asked were similar to those to which we might like an answer – "how likely is the stock market to fall by 20% next year?"

Have a look at the picture of a bell curve below. The line in the middle is the average or mean, in this case the average height of an American male, which you can see is 5'10". You can see that 68% of the time men's height falls 3 inches either side, that is 5'7"- 6'1" (called "one standard deviation"). And 95% of all men are 5'4"-6'4" (which is "two standard deviations").

Chart 1: The normal distribution of the US male population

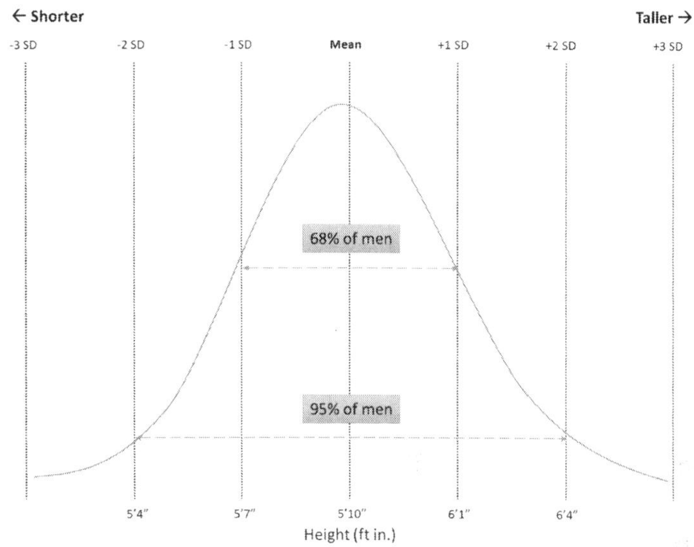

Then there is the incidence of three standard deviations, which is what happens only 0.3% of the time, so rarely. But bearing in mind the size of the U.S. male population, you can still predict that 28 men will be between 7'1" and 7'4".

This mix of different heights is what is called a "normal" distribution – and I emphasise "normal". In simple terms, it means certain extremes are not just improbable but impossible – for example, you cannot grow to be a mile in height.

A few people tinkered with this idea in an investment context (notably Louis Bachelier at the turn off the 19th century), but in the modern era, the first big step was taken in 1952.

Let's be clear. You have great potential when you invest. Let me show you.

If you invested £1,000 in the UK stock market in 1945, it would today be worth **£1,796,950.**

Left on deposit it would have grown to a mere £62,610.

The stock market provided returns more than **28x greater** – that is an extraordinary difference.

But 1945 was perhaps a favourable time to begin investing. What about shorter periods, more relevant to your timescales?

Well, based on over 100 years of data, if you stay invested in the UK stock market for 10 years there was a 91% likelihood that you would have achieved a better return than leaving your money on deposit.

91% probability not good enough?

Then if you left it invested for 18 years the odds increased to 99%.[11.]

Nonetheless, over that 18 years, the road had many twists and turns – this is volatility. Your investment journey if you like. Though history suggests that if you stick with this journey long enough there is a high probability (but not a certainty) that you will make decent money, there is no certainty as to what you will get back or when.

Until the 1950s (perhaps until the 1970/80s), a stockbroker would rely heavily on **gut feeling**, hoping that the journey (the day-to-day ups and downs of share prices) would not be too volatile in the short term, but in the expectation that if you hang in there all will come to good – just as the above numbers suggest.

Chicago, USA. 1952.

It should not be a surprise that some found this approach a tad woolly.

Cue an unknown 25-year-old student at the University of Chicago.

He was kicking his heels pondering a topic for his doctoral dissertation. He was waiting in a room to see his professor and "struck up a conversation with a stock broker" who urged him to help solve problems facing stock market investors, in particular better understanding the risks they were taking.

This student had no interest in investment matters, Bernstein tells us, and knew nothing of the stock market

His name was Harry Markovitz, a self-styled "nerd" student.[12]

In his paper *"Portfolio Selection"*, he set out to construct portfolios with "desirable" growth prospects but less volatility. This was admirable – after all who wouldn't want growth with less volatility, a smoother journey?

He rejected the idea of betting the ranch on one investment idea (though this can work as I will show you later) and instead focussed on smoothing out the journey for investors by diversifying e.g. while some stocks in the portfolio will be going down in value, others will be going up, making the average volatility lower.

It was a case of better managing what you could. Investors have no power over how an individual investment will turn out for them. But by combining lots of investments together, it is possible to reduce the risks or volatility of the whole, of the portfolio.

In one sense, what Markovitz did was hardly big news. The Dutch adventurer Van Ketwich had worked out that simple matter in 1774. Some ventures work, others won't. But you don't risk everything on one venture.

What was now different was that a single number could be put on that risk, and it was now possible to mathematically quantify the benefits of diversifying, of spreading your bets if you like.

He showed that investing is not simply about picking investments in isolation, but about picking the right *combination* of investments.

This combination of investments was not just a portfolio; with guidance from Markovitz's equations, it was also an *efficient* portfolio.

Maths replaced intuition or gut feeling.

Client portfolios which had been structured a bit "seat-of-pants" could now be "efficient".

If maths could guide investors and portfolio managers in this way to help prevent them taking unnecessary risks, Markovitz had certainly added some value.

But it was some time before this idea caught on, for a number of reasons.

Firstly, the maths was complex.

Secondly, to efficiently and cost-effectively create that efficient portfolio required access to computers which did not exist in 1950s.

Thirdly, why bother? This was an extraordinary and positive time, and fund managers became folk heroes in the 1960s.

Then in the early 1970s, markets came tumbling down, fund manager "skill" was exposed as the luck of riding a prolonged bull market, and the idea of better managing risk, the Markovitz idea, suddenly became more urgent.

Oh, and computer technology had moved on considerably.

Markovitz, our disinterested nerdy student, laid the foundation for not just the academic work which followed, but ideas which, from the 1970s, began to dominate the way that much of the finance industry worked.

For example, his idea was the efficient *portfolio* where, by properly combining certain investments, you could reduce your overall risks – an admirable idea. Then in 1965-1970, Eugene Fama came up with the idea of efficient *markets* – which put the cat amongst the pigeons.

Essentially, his **Efficient Market Hypothesis** meant we should all just invest into funds which mirror the performance of the stock market, index trackers, because:

- all investors are rational.
- all information is available to all of those investors at the same time.
- and because those investors are rational they all respond in much the same way.
- Therefore, market prices always reflect fair value.

This meant there is no point trying to do better than the stock market because, in the parlance, there are no inefficiencies – there are no angles which someone else hasn't already considered; there are no stones left unturned. That's the theory.

If he and his proponents had simply said "buy index trackers because the alternatives are not good enough", some might have said "fair enough". But they went much further with the idea that we are rational and all behave in the same way at all times – this is self-evident nonsense at various levels.

We know investors are not rational because, if they were, you could not get under- and over-valuation. You would not get investment bubbles, which are based on extraordinary over-confidence, and are inherently **not** rational – it is extreme emotions which clearly drive markets at extremes, whether they be highs or lows.

That emotions have such a pivotal role in driving markets has been well documented for a very long time. For example, the marvelous 19th century tome "*Extraordinary Popular Delusions and the Madness of Crowds*",[13] and more recently the sweeping historical review by the late Charles Kindleberger "*Manias, Panics and Crashes.*"[14]

But I'm getting ahead of myself.

Clues

- Very clever mathematicians, with no investment knowledge, begin to move centre stage.
- A maths model, not intended for the investment industry, was adopted by the investment industry.
- A theory of how markets work began to unfold.
- A number was put on risk.
- Maths could replace intuition or gut feeling.
- That gut feeling was not enough was made clear when markets tumbled (1970s).
- But this theory of rational markets clashed with what happened in the real world.

Next Steps

Mad maths...

5. Maths: The Solution Or The Problem?

We saw how child genius Carl Gauss did some clever, and useful, things with maths. We saw how his bell curve could help us organise, and make sense of, a jumble of statistics from day-to-day life and in nature.

But when you try and apply this to investment, it gets very difficult. Look at the following bell curve, similar in look to the one shown earlier. This is very elegant maths in a seductive picture.

Chart 2: The normal distribution of investment returns

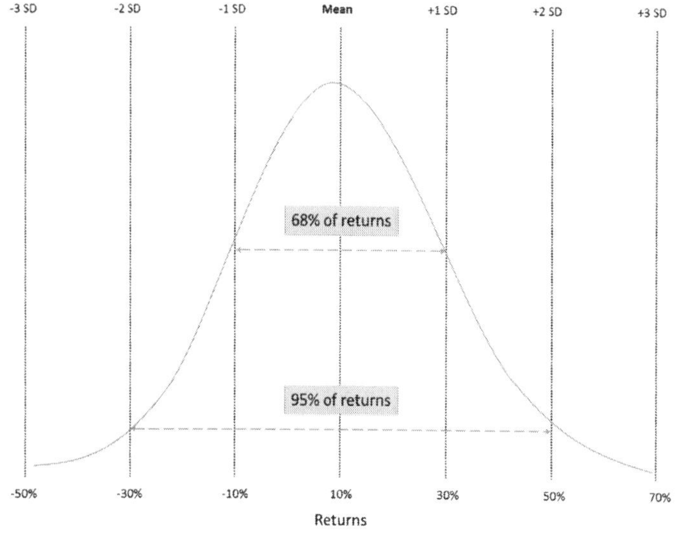

In this case, the line down the middle tells us that the average growth rate is 10% per annum, which is about right for the UK stock market.[15] The bell curve has organised the jumble of annual returns since 1900 to tell us that in 68% of individual years the return was within 20% of this average, so between 10% *down* and 30% *up*. (These are approximate numbers for illustration).

Taken a step further, it tells us that 95% of the time the price moved 40% either side of that average (so between -30% and +50%).

This is probability, guided by what happened in the past.

This is a useful guide when combined with other useful information: e.g. that over 18 years, you have a 99% probability of generating more growth than leaving your money on deposit. But it is only a guide.

You also need to factor in the bumps along the way in that 18-year journey, something to which I will return.

The problem is that many believe this bell curve has *predictive ability* – **it doesn't**, at least not in the context of financial markets. It is predictive in the context of the height of men driven by thousands of years of evolution. But not in the context of financial markets driven by the behaviour and idiosyncrasies of human beings.

Nonetheless, the (bad) idea that investment returns can be predicted in this way became the building block for very significant developments in the finance industry. At its simplest, it appeared that, armed with a good sample of past results, statisticians could predict future results with some confidence.

This laid the foundations for significant advances such as the Black-Scholes equation (1973) and VaR or value-at-risk (1994).

Black-Scholes "opened up a new world of ever-more-complex investments, blossoming into a gigantic global industry",[16] and underpinned massive economic growth. It was even called the *Midas Formula,* as it seemed to be a recipe for making everything turn to gold.

But the combination of muddled maths, complexity, greed, and leverage (debt) meant the finance industry was out of control. The scale of this was only truly apparent in 2007/8 with the sub-prime mortgage debacle,[17] the failure of Lehman Brothers, and the world moving to the brink of Great Depression II.

VaR was used by banks (and regulators) to measure risks being taken by banks, and, hopefully, to enable them to limit those risks. In the jargon, someone assessing risk could say "with 95% confidence" how much they might lose – or even with 99.7% confidence if required to appease regulators and shareholders.

But this created a false sense of security, even complacency.

The problem is that extremes occur commonly in financial markets. And this was not allowed for in the bell curve, the Black-Scholes equation, or VaR.

What this maths suggested was improbable was actually happening all the time! The maths disregarded the big market moves – but it was big market moves that would bring the banks and the whole system down.

For example, the sharp fall in the UK stock market in 1974 (down 57% after inflation) should only happen once in 1,400 years according to the maths. The 97% real return in 1975 should only happen once in 30,000 years.

It gets worse. The U.S. stock market's one-day fall in August 1997 had a probability of one in 50 billion. A week of steep falls in July 2002 had a probability of one in four trillion.

When the U.S. stock market fell 23% in a single day in 1987 this was, according to bell curve analysis, something which should only happen "once in several billion years" (or, for those still following the maths, a 22 standard deviation event – that is odds of 100 quindecillion, which is 100 followed by 48 zeros).

Or "odds so small they have no meaning", at least mathematically.[18]

Yet in the real world, such events have real meaning. They can have a dramatic and lifelong negative impact on your finances.

And sometimes they bring the whole global system to the brink, as when the maths models didn't anticipate the extraordinary crisis of 2008, which brought the world to the brink of Great Depression II. Even Queen Elizabeth felt obliged to ask: "why did nobody see it coming?" when she visited the London School of Economics (LSE) in November 2008.

Buckingham Palace, England. 2009

An A-list of academics and practitioners was convened to provide a considered opinion for the Queen, and it was published on 22nd July 2009. I have to admit that I tittered reading it. There are only two pages, and it mostly falls into the category of "the bleeding obvious". (There is a third full page, but this is just a list of the 33 worthies who contributed – that's an average of two-and-half lines each.) Here's a flavour:

> *Most believed the financial wizards had found new and clever ways of managing risks.... There was a belief too that financial markets had changed... It was a cycle fueled not by virtue but by delusion...The psychology of herding and the mantra of financial and policy gurus led to a dangerous recipe... The failure was principally a failure of the imagination of many bright people to understand the risks to the system as a whole"*

To be fair, these guys (there were no lady "experts") were remarkably frank – they realised that the Queen would not tolerate bluff and waffle.

Yet this could be a description of most financial crises of the last 300 years – which Mackay wrote about in 1841, and Kindleberger chronicled in detail from 1978 – both widely read books to this day. These lessons of history had never been taken on board by such bankers, governments and regulators – and they were of no interest to those who saw an opportunity to line their pockets, and damn the consequences.

Centuries of crises were fueled by greed, deception, delusion, herding, and easy availability of debt – oh, and on this occasion, bonkers maths.

The motion of the planets is a scientific matter, measurable with mathematical precision. The height range of males is dictated by millions of years of evolution, to maximise the chances of survival. In sharp contrast, financial markets (a very new development in the context of human evolution) are driven by human behaviour, which is not measurable with precision by any mathematical formula (bell curve or otherwise).

Investments are not "normal" in a way which can usefully be measured or represented by the bell curve. You can disregard the possibility of someone growing a mile high – it isn't even a possibility. But you can't disregard even a remote possibility in financial markets – in fact you have to allow for possibilities which have never been seen before, the acutely abnormal (a possibility which we build into your plan later in the book).

The problem was that investment models built on this kind of maths were (and are still) not just wrong, "they are dangerously wrong".

Here was laid the seed of an angry debate which still rages.

These theories bear no relationship to the real world of investing. They merely describe the past, and only a slither of the past, and cannot predict the future. Or in the case of the Efficient Market Theory, it doesn't even describe the real world, past present or future.

Some critics admit that these ideas have a degree of value, but it is limited – the numbers provide a useful guide but not more. The problem is that many were, and remain, seduced by the elegant maths and take these theories too far.

The critics tell us that these clever theorists might have extraordinary IQs, but have little common sense.

To be fair to Gauss, he never said that the bell curve had applicability to the stock market – it was in modern times that many people (and too many bright people) became seduced by his elegant maths.

Or as Keynes put it, as early as 1936:

> *Too large a proportion of recent 'mathematical' economics are merely concoctions, as imprecise as the initial assumptions they rest on, which allow the author to lose sight of the complexities and interdependencies of the real world in* ***a maze of pretentious and unhelpful symbols.***

And in the context of investment funds, which is our focus, these "concoctions" have led many investors just like you to adopt index trackers (or worse) and do themselves a huge injustice – you must avoid this trap. **You can do so much better than index trackers, as you will see.**

CLUES

- Mathematical models take no account of irrational investors and emotion-driven markets.
- Mathematical models take no account of extremes which are quite commonplace.
- Mathematical models encourage complacency.
- Elegant maths are seductive (even when wrong).
- The role of common sense and experience is considerably, and continually, under-estimated.

NEXT STEPS

By accident, "mad maths" shone a light on what did work.

6. Say 'Thank You' to a Daft Theory

The story so far...
In the 19th century, Gauss (and others) developed the maths on which others in the 20th century built the modern finance industry.

Notably, it was Markovitz, our disinterested nerdy student, who in 1952 developed the equations so investors could think about risk in a quantifiable way, and stop flying by the seat of their pants.

His idea was the efficient *portfolio*, whereby properly combining certain investments you could reduce your overall risks – an admirable idea.

By 1970, Eugene Fama came up with the idea of efficient *markets* – which put the cat amongst the pigeons. This assumed we are all rational and should just buy index trackers – because there are no angles which someone else hasn't already considered, there are no stones left unturned.

This is self-evident nonsense at various levels, as I made clear in chapter 4.

The good news is that this theory spawned an extraordinary volume of research into investment markets, exploring what makes them tick.

On the one hand, this research, and the experience of practitioners like myself, tends to show that most investors struggle to consistently do better than the stock market most of the time. This might be wealthy individuals buying shares, or fund managers, or investors buying funds. Our own research confirmed this, as set out in chapter 2 – and as you will see again later.

But, and this is a very important BUT, this volume of research also uncovered investment approaches or strategies, which DO consistently generate growth better than the stock market indices – in other words, much better than returns from merely being invested into index trackers, the funds which track the stock market.

Here are four of those approaches which this research illustrates consistently provide better returns:

- **Momentum investing.** This means, in simple terms, buying winners. Buying investments which are going up more than others because there is a tendency for that investment to continue performing well for a certain period of time – that this is the case has been well established in many academic papers since the 1930s from Yale to Harvard to London Business School.

- **Value investing.** Value investing is what Warren Buffet is famous for. Buy what can be identified as cheap without good reason, because one day that value will be recognised.
- **Small cap investing.** As the name implies, buying smaller companies, which have a tendency to be under-researched, and therefore have hidden value.
- **High yield investing.** Buying shares with an above average dividend yield, in particular with a payout which is sustainable and will grow.

Let's look at a bit more detail for each. In particular, I am interested in the extent to which YOU can buy funds to exploit these possibilities.

1. Momentum Investing

Momentum investing has been researched endlessly by a range of very big brains; what is clear is that investments which have done well recently have a tendency to keep doing well in the period ahead.

It is so straightforward it is almost insulting – it simply means buying winners; buying shares or funds which are doing best now on the assumption that they will continue doing well for a certain period of time. The long-term success of this approach has been documented over many decades by many different sources including ourselves[19]: e.g. one research paper by the London Business School in turn references another 61 pieces of research on Momentum investing.[20]

It is individual shares which have been the focus of this research (which probably now runs into thousands of papers). It has been conducted by very-well-regarded academic institutions from Harvard to London Business School. They tend to reach the same conclusion, not just on U.S. or UK stock markets, but considering an array of stock markets around the world over many decades – some also consider other asset classes, with similar results.

What none appear to have considered are investments into ***funds***, at least not until we did our detailed research – which I will return to shortly in detail *as it is VERY important for your investing success.*

2. Value Investing

This isn't about simply buying what is cheap, as a company might have a low share price for very good reasons. Rather it is buying what is unjustifiably cheap. So rather than buying a winner (Momentum investing), you are buying a certain kind of loser.

This requires that you have: the skill to analyse financial accounts, calculate a true market value, and identify an anomaly; great patience, as it could take years before the market reflects your analysis, if at all; great discipline, to keep applying this analysis in the years ahead; great temperament, so you don't get distracted by market woes along the way, let alone life's personal travails.

The problem with **Value investing** is that you can never know when the value hidden away in a share will be recognised by the wider market – it could be years. Hard work and patience are vital, but at a level which is untenable for most private investors. This approach is captured in some individual funds such as *M&G Recovery*, and a number of *Schroder* funds.

3. Small Cap Investing

This means investing into the dynamic heart of all successful economies.

From 1955 to 2016, smaller companies grew by 15.4% per annum, which was 3.6% more than the wider stock market.[21]

This extra growth per annum might not sound like much. But if those growth rates persisted in the next 20 years it would mean your portfolio or pension fund is 88% greater!

Put that another way – it could be an **88% pay raise** in retirement.

How does that sound?

Would you like to do even better?

This isn't even the best way to exploit the potential in smaller companies – it can be substantially better than this, as I will show you later – it only requires a couple of simple steps on your part.

Though smaller companies can suffer from notable periods of under-performance versus larger companies (such as a number of years in the 1990s), small cap funds offer extraordinary potential, assuming you have a process to select the right funds – more on that exact point later.

4. High Yield Investing

High yield investing is a strategy reflected in equity income funds, which invest into shares paying above average dividends. The key to the performance is the reinvestment of those dividends.

We know that over 10 year rolling periods since 1899, there is a 91% probability that investing in the UK stock market will perform better than leaving the money on deposit.

How about an investment strategy which meant you could do *even better* than that? 85% of the time?

To explore this possibility, Elroy Dimson and his colleagues at London Business School shared some raw data with us – their index of higher-yielding shares which goes back to 1900.

Our research then highlighted that, if you had adopted a high yield investing strategy since 1900, in 85% of 10-year rolling periods you would have generated even more growth than the stock market as a whole.[22]

Funds which exploit this strategy typically sit within the fund sectors called "UK Equity Income" and "Global

Equity Income" – though not all of them are successful in applying this simple approach.

Remember this is for growth investors and, in this case, the key to that growth is the reinvestment of income over long periods.

In contrast, building an income portfolio, to pay out income regularly, is a very different matter which I don't cover in this book. But we (FundExpert) do provide research and updates in this area, and have developed a fantastic and unique tool to help you make better choices.[23]

Long-term evidence

The evidence supporting these very distinct approaches to investing is compelling.

I want to introduce you to *"What Works on Wall Street"*, a very important book first published in 1996 and regularly updated since. The author, James O'Shaugnessy, sought to quantify these approaches to investment, and drove a cart and horses through the idea that markets are efficient and that the only investment solution is an index tracker. Though his numbers relate to the U.S. stock market, they equally apply to the UK.

Here is one staggering example from the latest edition.

An original investment of $10,000 in 1926 has grown to a sum nearly **10x** greater than the index if you used **Value** investing. That is extraordinary in itself. But much more extraordinary is the value of that $10,000 if you had used a simple **Momentum** strategy – it is more than **20x** greater than the index!

$10,000 invested in December 1926 [24]		
	Value in Dec 2009 ($)	Compound Annual Return
S&P 500	23,171,851	9.78%
Value Investing [24]	200,324,516	12.68%
Momentum Investing	572,831,563	14.11%

Obviously, the timespan shown here is much longer than you have in mind, so later I will be illustrating periods which are more relevant to you.

CLUES

- A volume of research reveals approaches to investment which generate returns consistently better than stock market indices (and by extension, index trackers).
- Some of these processes work for private investors buying funds, while others are more appropriate for the fund managers themselves.
- Puzzle – so why do investors and fund managers do so badly?

NEXT STEPS

We need to understand why the fund managers are failing to exploit the potential which O'Shaugnessy set out in huge and compelling detail, and see what lessons you can learn.

7. Are Fund Managers Stupid or Lazy?

THOSE LAST FEW chapters built a picture of the battleground between:

- Those who believe investors (including fund managers) cannot consistently beat the stock market – in which case you should buy index tracking funds.
- Those who believe the stock market is full of opportunity, largely because we are not rational investors – in which case you just need a process to identify outstanding investment opportunities (including actively managed funds).

But our research of fund manager failure begs the awkward question...

Are fund managers stupid or lazy?

As I mentioned early on, in the first chapter, the scale of fund manager failure provides plenty of raw material for us to explore.

Why do so many clever people appear to get it so consistently *wrong*?

If we can answer that question it will make it much easier to identify the ingredients you need to be consistently *right* i.e. achieve consistent above-average growth.

One noisy cohort of critics will tell you that these active fund managers cannot possibly outperform the markets because we are all rational, markets prices always reflect all information, and therefore there is no undervaluation to exploit (AKA the Efficient Market Theory which we considered earlier).

If this theory were true, there would be no point buying anything other than index trackers.

But this theory is daft. As I said earlier, if we were rational, we would not get panics and crashes, manias and bubbles. Share prices would not have many multiples more volatility than underlying company profits. And if professional investors were rational, you would not go into a City trading room and see people watching Bloomberg TV for ideas (which would be like visiting your GP as he watched Casualty on TV looking for treatment tips!).

If rational or efficient markets are not the reason why the great majority of fund managers consistently fail, what is?

Formulas for success are clear

The need for sound processes to achieve consistently outstanding returns has been understood for decades. For example, in 1934, a famous book by Graham and Dodd highlighted the tendency of investors to under-value companies that were out of favour, and set out how this could be exploited: *"Security Analysis"* was the foundation for Value investing.

Today, even more comprehensive and accessible research is available, such as *What Works on Wall Street* by James O'Shaughnessy. First produced in 1996, and regularly updated since, it forensically identifies strategies which have consistently generated superior investment returns for nearly 100 years – you saw a fantastic example at the end of the last chapter.

That such processes are well known and understood makes the dismal performance of so many funds even more puzzling.

There are two broad categories of problems – structural and behavioural.

Structural problems are those built into the nature of the industry:

Performance Pressure

Performance pressures aren't helpful. If you are a fund manager, don't ask the sales team why your fund isn't selling if you can't illustrate recent superior performance. This pressure encourages too much focus on short-term performance.

Too Many Meetings

Fund managers spend too much time in meetings explaining why they are "special" (irrespective of unimpressive recent performance) rather than being given the time and space to focus on running their funds.

Too Many Regulations

There are myriad regulations and restrictions, and they seem to continually expand, creating new layers of distractions. Many more restrictions are created by house rules and investment committees and in-house compliance departments.

Too Much Information

The very nature of markets is a distraction, both for fund managers and you and me. Frenzied in the short term, and always highly complex. It was always thus.

Plus, an extraordinary volume of information, vastly more in the internet age, means more distractions but no greater knowledge. There are just too many distractions for all but the most emotionally detached.

All these issues leave managers with a shortage of time to make key strategic decisions as well as better understand the stock-level analysis which they are being fed.

Remuneration Rewards Size Not Performance

The way many managers are paid doesn't help, as it tends to be based more on assets under management than investment success. If their pay was more dependent on their longer-term investing success, it would surely focus the mind somewhat better.

Career Risk

It is not easy (emotionally or commercially) to act against the consensus – but this is key to the success of Value investing. Acting against the crowd draws attention to you and, when you aren't firing on all cylinders, risks making you look stupid AND losing your job.

More generally, the risk of mistakes encourages conservative behaviour, which generates mediocre performance.

The BIG reason?

The big structural reason for failing funds is that achieving outstanding investment performance is not the priority of most fund management businesses.

That might sound strange, so let me explain.

Fund management companies are businesses set up to make profits for shareholders, just like any other. And it has privately been illustrated to me on a number of occasions that the most profitable fund businesses are NOT those with the most successful funds. The most profitable fund businesses are those with the biggest marketing budgets.

Big marketing budgets, telling good stories, and pressing the right consumer buttons will attract the largest inflows of funds from investors – the performance of underlying funds is secondary to a successful fund management business (notwithstanding pressures to perform, as mentioned earlier).

Potential investors are suckers for a good story! The best marketing directors know that.

The Solution?

It isn't for you or I to solve the problems of the fund management industry.

My brief, and your brief, is much simpler...

- Make sure that you do not repeat the mistakes of the fund managers.
- Identify how you can select the small number of funds with outstanding potential.

But how can we do that?

Perhaps the clues to the solution are inherent in the two reasons index trackers work to the extent to which they do:

- A **simple strategy** (buy the index constituents!)
- **No personal or emotional judgments** required

Simple strategies, other than simply buying the index, are well understood – O'Shaughnessy and others have made those strategies absolutely clear, and I have provided you with a volume of our own evidence too. These don't generate just a little bit more growth than index-trackers, but a life-changing amount.

What about emotional judgments?

This leads us to the second category of problems for fund managers, **behavioural**. The problem we all tend to share

Behavioural Finance – understanding the psychology of investment decisions

Behavioural finance is concerned with better understanding why we make investment decisions in practice, in contrast to economic models which tell us how we should make such decisions in theory, in a theoretical rational world – which has only limited practical value.

Though often cited as a new area of study it has long been understood that to understand markets you must understand the state of mind of investors into that market. This was covered off in 1841 by Charles Mackay's marvellous Extraordinary Popular Delusions and the Madness of Crowds. In 1912 came Psychology of the stock market by George Charles Selden. Others followed but the most important modern work began with Tversky and Kahneman in the 1970s and 1980s, and then in 1985 "Does the stock market overreact?" was published in The Journal of Finance (De Bondt and Thaler).

with managers of actively managed funds is the quality of our personal and emotional judgements – a behavioural problem.

Computers and algorithms now enable us to rapidly test, over many decades, what strategies work. These computers don't have egos or life distractions.

In contrast, we mere humans (whether private investors or fund managers) are a bundle of inconsistencies and emotions.

Consider these examples, starting with over-confidence in our own abilities.

Ask a number of people whether they consider themselves below, average, or above average car drivers and the majority will opt for "above average". We all tend to think we are above average, but that isn't statistically possible!

If those investors are also expert fund managers, they are *even more* inclined to have these problems, as are all "experts" – a worrying trend that has been empirically illustrated many times.

James Montier tells how he gets expert fund managers at his seminars to answer questions about themselves and their behaviour, and one is "Are you above average at your job?"[25]

He says "a stunning 75% of those asked think themselves above average at their jobs. Many have written such things as *'I know everyone thinks they are above average, but I am.'* "

Oh dear. Based on our research only about 8% are better than mediocre.

Yet in chapter 6, we saw that there are some simple, well-proven, processes which fund managers could apply and be consistently above average. Why is this not happening?

One of the great books on both economics and how we behave and think is *"Thinking Fast And Slow"*.[26] It asks the question: ***"why are experts inferior to algorithms?"***. Algorithm is maths-speak for a straightforward process – sometimes a process which is no more than a checklist.

The answer? **Experts try to be clever – too clever**. They want to think outside the box and come up with complex solutions. Occasionally complex solutions work, but typically you will get a worse outcome than applying a simple process whose effectiveness is well-proven by evidence.

Experts, including fund managers, typically believe that they can overrule a simple formula because they have some additional insight – usually they don't.

You might say intellectual snootiness makes it difficult for managers to embrace simpler solutions which are empirically proven (such as **Momentum**), because these solutions aren't sufficiently intellectually challenging. After all, as an expert, surely you should be adding some value? Otherwise you look dumb.

This is a common problem, and it goes beyond intellect – there is simply a bias to take action. Football penalty kicks are a good example.

A large study[27] showed that if goalkeepers simply remained stationary in the middle of the goal they would sharply increase their chances of saving a penalty kick. Why don't they change their behaviour? Because this shot-stopping expert feels a compulsion to be seen to do something – and standing still makes it appear that you aren't trying.

Way back in the 1920s, legendary investor Jesse Livermore well understood the problem:

> *"After spending many years in Wall Street and after making and losing millions of dollars I want to tell you this: it was never my thinking that made the big money for me. It always was my sitting."*

Glorious inactivity.

Do you look at the prices of your investments far too often? Are you buying and selling and switching regularly but with little obvious benefit? This is the compulsion to act in action – it is a very unhelpful investment trait.

Fear of losses is another deep-seated problem, again highlighted by Daniel Kahneman way back in 1979.[28] In a nutshell, we may like to win but we hate to lose. Losing is painful. It means we admit a mistake, and we will go to great lengths to avoid that feeling.[29]

As a result, we all tend to hold onto losing investments, and sell winners – a very costly error. This applies just as much to fund managers as you and me. This was confirmed in a huge study of 30,000 funds in the U.S.[30] An earlier study of private investors showed that the subsequent performance difference between the winners sold and the losers held amounted to 3.4% per annum – that is a big performance hit if repeated year after year.[31]

Fund managers are smart people; have no doubt about that. When they buy a stock, the best of them will have trawled over that company and have very clear reasons for buying. But my experience of three decades is that they struggle to know when to sell.

I have often asked fund managers: "will you sell if a stock falls by a certain amount?". The typical response is something like "if the facts change". Woolly. I usually follow up with: "why don't you sell when the stock falls by a certain amount?" (AKA a stop-loss). No one does. So, when might that fund manager believe his original analysis is wrong? After it has fallen 10%? Or 20%? 50%?

Yet, in contrast, I often hear "I sold xyz stock because it hit my price target". Hmmm. Selling winners, holding losers. And that's the pros.

Most fund managers aren't stupid or lazy, but they are often overwhelmed by these human frailties (which we all share to some degree). So, even when a fund manager is focussed on achieving outstanding performance, basic human frailties will regularly knock him or her off course, resulting in failure to consistently beat undemanding benchmarks.

We know many fund managers who express a clear strategy. But either there is no empirical reason to believe it will work OR it is simply not consistently applied over time, for all the reasons set out above.

And therein lies the key to the success of private investors – **discipline** – that is the discipline to consistently apply a proven process.

Or as Goethe said, "in the real world all rests on perseverance".

This is what you can learn from the failure of fund managers – the need for a **process,** and the discipline to apply it consistently. Discipline is the harder part, but we have developed a straightforward solution, as you will discover shortly.

Moreover, the solution is much easier for you for two reasons:

1. You can succeed because you are incentivized like no one else – because it is your money.
2. You can do this by investing just 30 minutes of your time twice a year – I will explain how later.

CLUES

- Rational markets do not exist, so this cannot be the reason why fund managers fail.
- Processes to successfully invest are both understandable, readily available and well evidenced...
- ...but a range of ***structural*** problems mean that managers do not have the time or incentive to consistently apply those processes.
- In addition, fund managers suffer a number of ***behavioural*** problems (which they share with us all) resulting in a lack of discipline.
- Profitability of fund groups is driven by marketing budgets, not fund performance.

NEXT STEPS

In the next two chapters, I want to move the focus firmly to you, and away from fund managers – it will start with a little homework.

8. How Do YOU Choose Funds Now?

Grab a pen and a bit of paper, or use the blank page opposite, and quickly write down how you choose funds now.

To help you focus, perhaps concentrate on just one fund, and write the name of that fund at the top, and the reasons underneath – one or two key words will do it if you're itching to read on.

If you *really* want to start making progress right now, if you are feeling *really* honest, why not pick on one of your larger fund holdings where you already have a strong sense that it was not bought for good reason?

You don't have to put the reasons in any particular order, though highlight the most important one if you can.

Do try and do this as honestly as possible as I will later ask you to revisit your answer.

A WORD OF CAUTION

If just doing this feels like hard work, and you are inclined to turn the page, I must caution you.

Before you can improve your current investing results, you need to acknowledge what you are currently doing (for better or worse)...

...otherwise you will likely struggle to achieve the consistent investment success which you desire.

Go for it! Just scribble down the main reason why you chose one of your funds – just one or two key words will do it. I will return to this.

9. I Know This Is a Rude Question But...

ARE YOU STUPID or lazy? If we can ask that question of the fund managers (who you might think are fair game), shouldn't that question also be asked of private investors buying funds or other investments?

After all, there is clear evidence of persistent failure by private investors, year after year. I will come back to the evidence on that shortly, to leave you in no doubt.

Why do most private investors (people like you and me) consistently fail to achieve consistent success? Whether using funds or shares. And whether as a novice investor with £20,000 or an experienced investor with a £1m+ portfolio.

DIY investors have a number of problems.

For a start, nearly all of us lack the most basic schooling on financial matters in general, and in investing in particular. Our children and grandchildren are in the same position – ironically just when the government is starting to pass responsibility for managing pension provision to the masses. (At a personal level, I am fortunate. I have been able to fill that knowledge gap by virtue of my "day job" for the last 30 years.)

This lack of financial education has allowed a volume of myths to flourish and many bad habits to go uncorrected.

All is not lost! The education issue can easily be solved, hence this book and our other initiatives.

But there is a bigger problem.

I have said this many many times over the years to DIY investors (and it also applies to advisers), and I keep repeating it in the hope that at some point I will be believed.

YOU are the biggest barrier to your success, even once the education issue has been tackled. This is because we are naturally bad at investing.

How do I know?

Partly because I have been doing this for a long time, and have made plenty of mistakes myself, but I have also observed the same mistakes made by others, and they are continually repeated.

Plus, my own experience has been confirmed in great detail and with impressive methodology by advocates of **Behavioural Finance (see note on page 65)**, which developed to counter the ideas of Fama and the "index-trackers or nought" crowd. A key figure in this new way of thinking about investing is Daniel Khanemann who received the Noble Prize in 2002 for his ground-breaking research.

Be absolutely clear, I am not a psychologist. But I have invested a lot of time trying to understand from some great psychologists and behavioural experts why you (and I) are so *naturally* bad at investing. Don't despair, there are solutions.

An early word of warning. The next bit might be old hat to you. Or you might say: "it's very interesting, but why is it relevant to me? Is it just padding to get the book's word count up?"

You are such a cynic! This is **very** important. If you don't grasp the essence of the problem outlined in this section the odds on your long-term investing success fall sharply.

The first thing to understand is that our brain and how it functions have evolved at a glacial pace.

This means that our brains are superbly constructed to deal with the African savannah 200,000 years ago, or the threats from the wilderness which was Europe 50,000 years ago, variously populated by hippopotami, rhinoceroses, mammoths, elephants, and the sabre-toothed tiger.

But our brain isn't so well adjusted to the industrial age, which began 250 years ago, and which began to turn the daily lives of those recent ancestors upside down.

And how about the "*internet age*" that we are now living through? You can be confident our brains aren't designed to cope with this age of superfast and ever-changing news and data.

What our brains are designed for is to maximise our chances of survival as the world existed 50-200,000 years ago.

Our brain, let's call it our *old* brain, learnt to take shortcuts, which meant it could respond rapidly to threats and improve the odds of survival. It is fast, a "quick and dirty" system, which enables your brain to take shortcuts with very limited information.

This is my favourite example of the old brain in action.[32]

- I place a glass box on the table in front of you.
- Behind the glass walls, it contains a large snake.
- I ask you to lean forward and concentrate on the snake.
- Suddenly it rears up!
- You WILL jump backwards.

That is your old brain in action. It will react to keep you safe – even though the snake is behind a glass barrier.

This is what happened. When the snake moved TWO signals were sent to your brain:

- One went on the fast road,
- One went on the slow road.

The fast road is straight to the old brain which deals with fear and risk and uncertainty.

There is a threat, and uncertainty, and the *old* brain jumps into action rapidly, and forces the body to move backwards rapidly – without hesitation.

In contrast, the signal that went more slowly, to what we might call the *new* brain, processed the information more consciously and recognised that there was a layer of glass between you and the snake. The new brain is more rational, but slow.

But the signal from the new brain of no threat was too late, you had already jumped backwards.

From a survival point of view, if you had been on the savannah thousands of years ago (*without* the benefit of the layer of glass) this old brain function is fast and effective – and would have saved your life. You would have died if you relied on the (slow) new brain to figure what to do.

Remember, the old brain acted on limited information, because it means it can react more quickly to less information. Are speed of response, and these shortcuts, always going to be helpful in the internet age? Let's see.

Consider this example in a modern context.

- Imagine you are walking into a shoe shop,
- you have your eye on a certain pair of shoes, and the price is OK.

- Then they announce you can have it for half-price,
- a Sale has just begun!

Wow. How can you refuse!

Perhaps you will even buy two pair.

It doesn't take the rational *new* brain long to figure that out.

In contrast now imagine:

- You are visiting your financial adviser,
- and you intend to invest a certain amount in a stock market fund.
- He enters the room, and announces that share prices have halved.

What do you do?

You run a mile!

In the first example, instant happiness. There is no threat from a half-price pair of shoes! What you see is what you get.

In the second example, instant fear. Without a second thought.

What was going on?

When you buy an investment you literally buy future uncertainty.

An investment is bought *in the hope* that you can sell it at a higher price, to make a profit. There is no certainty that you will make a profit.

Unhelpfully from an investment perspective, our brain is designed, hard-wired, to react in a very distinct way when confronted with uncertainty.

When there is the sort of sudden price change we saw above, the future uncertainty is immediately crystalised, as if someone has just hit you over the head.

Our impulse, is to retreat – flight.[33] Flight means you survive, you live to fight another day.

In addition, if the price is falling sharply, a lot of investors are selling, doing the opposite of what you were considering. This instinctively makes you feel very uncomfortable. This is because you (and all of us) have a VERY strong instinct to herd – our experiences on the savannah taught us that to be in a herd brings safety.

As soon as you know prices have halved and the herd is running in the opposite direction to you, your very strong instinct is to join that herd, because it is safer.

The *old* brain still dominates your behaviour, even in this modern investment context. **This is very unhelpful**. So, a good starting point for your future investing success is to acknowledge that you have these unhelpful traits – because it will make it easier to adopt the solutions.

Fear vs Greed

We are a bundle of hormones and instincts which don't always sit easily together. Fear and greed are two powerful instincts.

Most of our lives are spent with confidence in the vanguard – it ebbs and flows of course, but at some level confidence oils our existence from day to day.

If some uncertainty arises (in an investment context or otherwise), the level of confidence will ebb, but it will rebuild, though often slowly.

At either end of this spectrum of confidence are **fear** and **greed**.

Greed emerges occasionally as confidence boils over. In investment terms, this is where bubbles come from – investment manias, which I'll look at again in a moment.

But *greed* doesn't come from nowhere. It builds over time as confidence grows, and eventually bubbles over into greed.

In contrast, ***fear*** **can come from nowhere** – as in the very basic example above when the value of the stock market fell and the aspiring investor instantly ran a mile with his money.

While confidence ebbs and flows, occasionally punctuated by greed, fear is under control most of the time, caged if you like.

But when something suddenly triggers fear, it runs amok and tramples any prior confidence, especially any greed instinct.

Therefore, we can say that confidence persists for long periods, and builds slowly, but fear emerges fast, and triggers evasive action. In an investment context, this often means rapid, emotional selling and typically poor decision-making. Even if we don't sell, this fear drowns out the new brain, and the possibility of a rational response to this new uncertain environment e.g. bargain hunting.

In addition, we are all subject to the problems observed in chapter 7 – such as over-confidence, and selling winners and holding onto losers.

So, are most of us stupid or lazy, in the context of investing?

The point is that we might be both very clever and hard-working, but we suffer from a number of in-built frailties. These so-called mental biases are there for very good reasons in an evolutionary context – but they are very unhelpful when you and I are investing.

A key part of this book is finding solutions to these frailties.

CLUES

- There is clear evidence of persistent failure by private investors.
- There is a lack of basic schooling on financial matters.
- Many bad habits go uncorrected...
- ...which is not helped because we are naturally bad at investing.
- The latter arises from our behaviour being dominated by our "old brain", which deals with uncertainty and risk.
- Plus we have a very strong instinct to herd, which encourages panic when uncertainty emerges – the flight instinct.
- Confidence builds slowly, but fear can come from nowhere.
- We need a process to prevent bad decisions when faced with uncertainty.

NEXT STEPS

I want to show how the ebb and flow of confidence, and fear and greed, literally shapes the stock market – and the evidence of investors struggling.

10. Anatomy of a Bull

In the last chapter, you saw that we have an unhelpful brain.

Confidence lubricates our day-to-day life.

But when we encounter uncertainty, we are inclined to run away – which is helpful when confronted with an elephant, but not when we experience a falling stock market.

In addition, I proposed that confidence builds slowly, but fear can emerge from nowhere (as our *old* brain jumps into action).

Now I would like you to observe this in action in the stock market.

You can see on this chart that when the stock market is rising it tends to do so steadily. But falls are sudden, and crushing.

Chart 3: The performance of the FTSE 100 index from 1994 to 2004

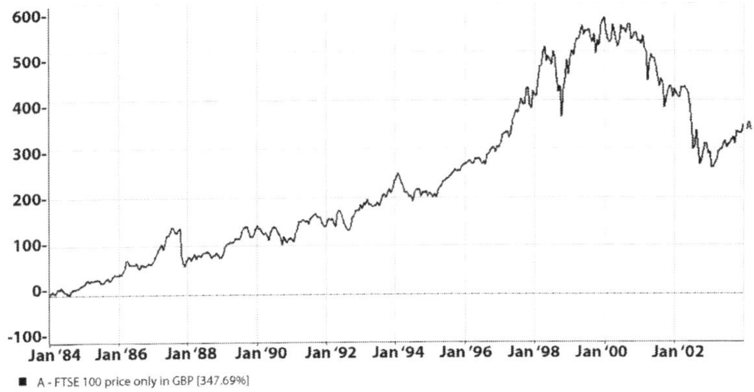

The relatively sedate upward trend is fed by a stream of new buyers over time – this stream of new buyers arises because ***confidence does not build uniformly across all investors***. People join the herd of investors at different times. This is self-evident from the steady incline of the chart from 1988 to 1998.

That upward trend will grow gradually *most* of the time. An exception occurs towards the end of some upward trends as confidence morphs to over-confidence and then out-and-out greed. The technology bubble of the 1990s is a great example. On the same chart above, you can see how the upward gradient sharply increases before the peak in 1998 and again in late 1999, before it all comes tumbling down, triggered by the technology crash.

[If you wish to look at this bubble in more detail, I have produced a history of that period – for a complimentary copy, go to **FundExpert.co.uk/techbubble***.]*

The herd of investors is a very mixed group. It is made up of powerful institutions and hedge funds (the so-called smart money) as well as retail investors. This herd is very powerful, fueling bull markets that can go on for years. It is the retail investors who tend to get to the party late in the day, when the upward trend is long established and the easy money has been made. And so it was in 1999/2000 as we document in our history – do get your complimentary copy of this.

In particular, it is those who are least-well-informed and ordinarily least-confident who will tend to join the herd late in the day. This is ironic because the higher the market goes, the more over-valued it becomes, and the greater the risks. But those late-in-the-day do not see this – they just take comfort from the safety of the herd – a caveman instinct, wholly inappropriate when investing.

It is bizarre, but true nonetheless, that complacency grows as prices go up – just as the market becomes more expensive and more dangerous.

I recall in 1999 I had a call from a lady journalist at the Daily Telegraph, who was writing a piece on the technology fund boom – she was definitely in the skeptic camp. I talked about the dangers and clear over-valuation and crazy investor behavior, which we were observing almost daily. Quite a large piece appeared the following weekend in the Telegraph. To my amazement, it was a long list of my peers confidently proclaiming there was no problem, and more to go for! At the very end of 5 columns, it eventually said "But Brian Dennehy warns...".

In addition, in March 2000, I told our clients:

> *"These speculators will be destroyed once a REAL correction gets underway, and that is a certainty."*

Over the next three years, tech funds fell in the region of 80-90%.

Not one of our advised clients had an exposure to technology funds – not one client, not one tech fund.

Terrible timing

The events of the late 1990s are just one example of the terrible timing of investors, who (but for panicking when fear prevails) are horribly slow to respond to unfolding events.

This problem is tracked by the *Dalbar Report*[34] in the U.S. every year.

For example, equity investors lost 4.66% EVERY YEAR over the last 20 years compared to being in a plain index tracker (tracking the S&P 500). That is an extraordinary loss of growth, year after year.

This was separately confirmed in the *Credit Suisse Investment Returns Yearbook 2014*. They noted that, in the 20 years ending in 2013, the return of individual investors was roughly 60-80% of that achieved by the market. They call it the "dumb money effect" and tell us:

> *"The root of the problem is bad timing... When markets are down investors are fearful and withdraw their cash. When markets are up they are greedy and add more cash"*

Again, the root of the problem is the ordinary investing public joining the herd far too late – buying high, selling low. This isn't because investors were trying to be clever – but rather they lacked *sufficient* confidence to buy earlier. Once the herd has grown substantially, and the market is already a long way ahead, only then will many investors jump on board.

Understanding that this is how profitable uptrends build is very important – it points us in the direction of an investment approach which exploits the herd, and will get you on board relatively early. Keep that thought in mind – it will be very important to your future success, and I will be returning to it shortly.

CLUES

- Confidence builds at a different pace amongst the individuals and institutions who make up the herd of investors.
- This fuels a steady rise in the stock market over time (a bull market), as different people have the confidence to buy at different times.

- In contrast, fear emerges rapidly across the herd of investors, and the stock market falls quickly (a bear market).
- Those who are least-well-informed and least-confident will tend to invest in the stock market (join the herd) late in the day.
- Complacency amongst investors tends to grow as prices go up, which is ironically when the stock market becomes more expensive and more dangerous.
- There is need for a process which helps you invest sooner.

NEXT STEPS

Let's see how one gentleman, the hero of our story, stumbled across a way to invest into funds with extraordinary success, while also side-stepping the very human limitations we have observed in the last two chapters.

11. The Mystery of the Missing £808,446

[This is the original written in 2014]

This is the story of the missing £808,446.

Someone lost this money. It might have been you.

But there is a happy ending. Because you (and I) can learn how to get it back in the years ahead, just like the hero of this story.

The story begins twenty years ago in 1994. At the time, the FTSE 100 index was at 3,418. In 1987, there had been an unpleasant interruption in an uptrend which began in 1974, but even this Crash was very short-lived, and the UK stock market continued its long term uptrend.

So 1994 did not represent an obviously cheap-as-chips time to buy equity investments. But the hero of our story had £100,000 to invest – he had inherited

£200,000 but decided to leave £100,000 on deposit, interest rates not being too terrible at the time.

Our hero, let's call him Harry, was not a patient man and simply wanted to invest the money. He knew a little about investing, through investing much smaller sums, and enjoyed reading around the subject, particularly biographies of legendary investors.

George Soros and Warren Buffett were living legends. And he read a number of intriguing books on investment history. "*Extraordinary Popular Delusions and the Madness of Crowds*", "*Manias Panics and Crashes*", and "*Where Are The Customers' Yachts?*". He was endlessly curious.

One book was particularly interesting and totally uncompromising – "*A Random Walk Down Wall Street*", by Burton Malkiel, first published in 1973.

The message of the book, written in a pithy style, was clear. There is no point buying anything other than index tracking funds (so-called passive funds) because actively managed funds are so poor, and the few good ones are inconsistent. This was the Fama doctrine which we mentioned in chapter 4 – the Efficient Market Hypothesis.

Harry could not bring himself to agree. Though not a very experienced investor, this didn't feel right. He couldn't PROVE it, but instinctively he felt there must be investors who can achieve consistently better returns than merely being invested in mind-numbing index trackers. And surely the success of the likes of Soros and Buffett proved this point, unless you believed they were merely extraordinarily lucky.

Harry had two advantages.

His tinkering with investing smaller sums in individual shares, usually following other people's tips, had been fascinating, but ultimately not terribly profitable – ring any bells? An occasional success would convince him he had turned the corner, and that he had some skill (rather than just being lucky), but it was invariably followed by a failure. It was fascinating but frustrating. Being brutally honest with himself, **he realised he had no special investment skill.**

Added to this conclusion was another edge – he did not like wasting his time, and **he was very disciplined by nature.**

So, spurred on by the £100,000 burning a hole in his pocket, he put the investment approaches of Soros and Buffett side by side for comparison. They were very different.

Buffett is what is called a Value investor. Through in-depth analysis of individual companies, he would identify the share prices of companies which were not just cheap, but unjustifiably cheap. The problem is that after you buy you have no idea when the market will eventually recognise that same value – considerable patience is required.

In contrast, Soros applied a type of Momentum investing. At its simplest, momentum investing means buying what is going up most today, on the assumption that it will keep going up tomorrow – a volume of research indicated this tendency *over certain timescales.* Harry was particularly impressed by a gentleman called David Ryan. He won the U.S. Investing Championship in 1985 with a 161% profit in one year! He came second in 1986 with 160% profit and followed that up with another first-place finish and yet another triple-digit return.

Ryan used such a strategy and said: "The more disciplined you can get, the better you are going to do."

Value investing seemed like very hard work, and Harry, still brutally honest, didn't feel he had the time or skills to research individual shares.

But **Momentum** investing appealed. He didn't need to have a view on the markets – which was good because he was honest enough to recognise that his view had no more validity than that of anyone else.

Rather than buying individual stocks, he figured that fund managers were already doing all of the hard work. Although not instinctively comfortable with the conclusions of Malkiel, he accepted that few fund managers were consistently successful – this was a statistical fact. But a good number were successful over shorter periods – again accepted, even by Malkiel.

So why not apply a Momentum strategy to buy funds? This would mean buying individual funds when they were flying high, and automatically dumping them when they weren't.

Eureka.

This was his plan. He wanted to stick to funds invested into the UK stock market; he felt a bit more comfortable with this domestic bias. So, in July 1994 he did this:

- Bought the best UK growth funds of the last 6 months.
- He planned to sell these 6 months later...
- ...and then buy the top performing funds of the then most recent 6 months.
- And he would repeat this process every 6 months.

These were the funds he bought and sold in the first 18 months:

July 1994 bought:	January 1995 bought:	July 1995 bought:
GAM UK Diversified	Halifax UK Growth	Halifax UK Growth
Fidelity Special Situations	Investec UK Special Situations	Jupiter UK Growth
Fidelity UK Select	Newton UK Equity	Aberdeen UK Mid Cap Equity
(sold 6 mths later)	*(sold 6 mths later)*	*(sold 6 mths later)*

Nothing too horrible happened until the Autumn of 1997. Then an economic crisis in Asia caused the UK stock market to fall by 11%[35] in six weeks.

There was a more serious repeat of this in Autumn 1998, with the Russian financial crisis of August followed by the collapse of the U.S. hedge fund LTCM.

Harry was unmoved, partly because he was just too busy to react to these world events. He kept it simple and just continued to apply his Momentum strategy, switching into the three top-performing funds every 6 months.

When the markets fell in this period, he appeared to perform no worse than anyone else – even at worst, he remained in substantial profit since his 1994 starting point.

The next three years were a little crazy. The tech bubble really gathered pace, dragging up the whole UK stock market. The FTSE 100 index hit a peak in December 1999 (which had still not been surpassed by 2014).

Then it all came tumbling down.

The technology investment bubble burst and the stock market fell 48% over the next three years.

That Harry remained too busy in his day-to-day life to panic was a fortunate coincidence – he didn't get distracted. Yet, he also consoled himself knowing that his Momentum strategy never got him into technology funds (which were in a different sector to his UK growth funds).

The world was not going to end, and his historical knowledge of previous similar episodes illustrated that such periods come and go – you just need to hold your nerve.

Even when market fell at its worst (down 48%),[366] the value of Harry's three-fund portfolio was still way above the 1994 value, by more than £134,000.

By 2003, a new market upswing had begun, and a very profitable 5 years lay ahead. The Momentum strategy was superb at keeping him in the very best funds. Over these next 5 years, the FTSE 100 went up 130% (with income reinvested), but Harry's portfolio went up by 206%.[37]

Markets had another surprise in store.

There were various warning signs that all was not well in 2007 - remember Northern Rock in the UK? In September 2008, the debt edifice came tumbling down when Lehman Brothers went bust, and the UK stock market fell by 31% from 15 September 2008 to 3 March 2009.[39]

At its worst, Harry's portfolio value fell to £332,860 – still a long way above the £100,000 invested in 1994, and £161,590[39] more than if he had been invested in an index tracker since inception.

The reason I have set out those major downward lurches over that 20 years is to illustrate that this was no easy time for investing – there were a very unusual number of ugly market falls. Yet Harry's approach remained extraordinarily successful.

Here are the key facts:

- As of February 2014, the value was **£1,179,114, up 1079%**.
- This was **3 times more than the index** had grown since 1994.
- An investment into the average UK growth fund would have grown to a mere **£370,668**...

- ...in comparison Harry generated an extra **£808,446**

	Initial (£)	End (£)	Return	Your Loss vs Harry (£)
Harry's portfolio	100,000	1,179,114	1079%	
UK stock market	100,000	454,000	354%	- 725,114
Sector average fund	100,000	370,668	271%	**- 808,446**

But unless you had the discipline and honesty of Harry, this £808,446 was lost to you.

In fact, the vast majority of investors lost out on that £808,446. We know that because:

- 92% of funds are mediocre at best *(our own FundExpert research).*
- Year after year, individual investors consistently generate substantially less than the stock market as a whole *(Dalbar Report).*
- Individual investors consistently buy high and sell low, missing out on significant profits *(Credit Suisse Yearbook 2014).*

Harry had stumbled across selecting funds by using a Momentum approach.

So *why* was Harry so rare in his success? Let me deal with that shortly.

Firstly, I want to emphasise three things:

1. **Harry didn't take daft risks.** He simply made (hugely) better choices from amongst mainstream funds invested into the UK stock market. I am going to show you how to do this.
2. **Harry's impressive result was certainly no fluke.** To prove this, shortly I explore how you (or Harry) would have performed if you invested at the worst time ever – even worse than he encountered from 1994 as we explored above.
3. Harry might be a fictitious DIY investor, but **his achievements are there for the taking**.

CLUES

- Harry was disciplined and patient.
- Many funds fail to beat a basic benchmark over longer periods, but a good number are very successful over shorter periods.
- **Value** investing is hard work for private investors...
- ...but **Momentum** investing isn't.
- Harry adopted the idea of Momentum to choose funds.

NEXT STEPS

Across these chapters, I have accumulated a lot of clues as to why those vast sums have gone missing – and how you might do vastly better. In the next chapter, I want to briefly pull that together.

After that, building on Harry's success, I want to introduce you to a unique development – a vital building block for your success.

12. Elementary

You and I have sought clues to the mystery of vast sums going missing – the disappearing growth.

Early on, I said that the scale of mediocrity should provide plenty of raw material for us to explore as we try and understand why so many clever people appear to get it so consistently *wrong*. More to the point, this will make it easier for us to identify the ingredients you need to be consistently *right*.

In this chapter, I want to briefly pull together the most important points we have uncovered so far, before moving on to the "nuts and bolts" part of the book.

From the beginning in the 18th century, funds gave ordinary people the chance to generate much better returns on their money, by enabling them to participate in dynamic businesses, not just in their own country but anywhere in the world.

If you invest for a long enough period, you should make handsome returns compared to leaving your money on deposit. But the journey can get unpleasant, and the investment industry and investors are very bad at either anticipating these or acting rationally in response to them.

If you make the right choices you can transform your financial future.

You must have a method to consistently select outstanding funds, as 92% of funds cannot beat a basic performance target most of the time.

The good news is that there are well-established ways to consistently achieve outstanding returns.

These solutions do not require special skills or experience on your part, nor involve you in taking any additional risks.

You must have a plan which sets out your method to select funds, and which also helps overcome other hurdles to your success:

- A tendency to act too slowly, particularly to embrace opportunities.
- A tendency to over-confidence and then panic.
- A tendency to be distracted by irrelevant detail.
- A tendency not to stick to a plan.

You need to think about your investment journey, and how you will respond to the ups and downs along the way.

You must avoid any theory of investment or elegant mathematical formula which has no basis in the real world; this is dangerous to your wealth.

You must avoid any investment idea which, though often and loudly repeated, has no evidence supporting it beyond proclamation.

You must only focus on a certain detail when there is solid evidence over many years that this single piece of information will help you identify funds with outstanding potential.

NEXT STEPS

You must have a straightforward plan which allows for all of the above – this will reduce stress, save you time, and stop you panicking at the first sign of trouble.

I am going to help you do that now, in the second half of our journey.

Choosing funds is certainly not the first step in that plan – but you must have a very robust method for selecting funds or the plan has no value. I am now going to introduce you to a unique development – a vital building block for *your* success.

PART II

13. Say "HELLO" to Dynamic Fund Ratings

You were introduced to our *Vintage Fund Ratings* back in chapter 2.

Now Harry has introduced us to another straightforward basis for selecting funds with even greater potential, and I want to show you how you can easily exploit that huge potential.

In the beginning

It is worth repeating a point made in chapter 11. Even Malkiel, a high priest of index trackers and the idea of efficient markets, recognised that at any one time there will be funds doing very well. Harry, the hero of our story, also recognised this.

With this in mind, in 2005 we began 5 years of VERY detailed research covering the period from 1994. We analysed 144 five-year rolling periods for all funds across all sectors.

The period 1994-2010 was by no means all gung-ho for markets. It included the bursting of arguably the biggest stock market bubble in history in December 1999, which was followed by an ugly three-year bear market – plus another ugly bear market in 2008/2009 and the greatest economic and financial market turmoil since the Great Depression. So, we certainly didn't research a conveniently bullish period.

The fund rating services which I had encountered since the 1980s were lacking, to say the least. So, if we at FundExpert were going to come up with a successful method for rating funds, I was conscious that this process MUST have these criteria:

- Straightforward to identify top-rated funds.
- The underlying process must be clear and understandable.
- It must be repeatable.
- There must be long term evidence of it generating extra growth.

The results

We back-tested various methods for selecting funds back to 1994. The method which stood head and shoulders above alternatives was what we now call ***Dynamic Fund Ratings,*** which reflects the approach which Harry used in chapter 11.

Dynamic Fund Ratings met all of our criteria for an effectivc rating system:

- **The funds to buy are given 5 stars. Couldn't be more straightforward.**
- **The 5-star funds are the top 20% of funds over the prior 6 months. That's clear.**
- **It is easy to repeat this process every 6 months.**
- **The evidence for achieving extra performance is superb.**

I repeat, we analysed 144 five-year periods for EVERY fund in EVERY sector. *[Technical point. Some of you might say "how come 144 five-year periods?". This is because every month since 1994 we began a new five-year period – so strictly speaking there are 144 overlapping five year periods.]*

Here is a table showing the EXTRA growth on average over five-year periods for four popular sectors from 1994-2011 (the period for our original Dynamic research). The third column also shows the likelihood of you outperforming the sector average in any of those 144 five-year periods.

Sector	EXTRA growth (over 5 years)	Likelihood of extra growth
UK All Companies	**50%**	*94%*
UK Smaller Companies	**90%**	*98%*
Global	**66%**	*96%*
Europe (excl UK)	**42%**	*99%*

The extra growth over such relatively short periods is impressive enough. The likelihood of you doing better than the average fund is even more impressive – all in excess of 90%.

This scale of extra growth can be life-changing.

The ***Dynamic Fund Rating*** system has produced some staggering results. Here is a breakdown of more recent results to July 2016 for the UK All Companies sector, now analysing 204 five-year periods since 1994. The results are impressive.

- **7.85% EXTRA** growth per annum – achieved by the *Dynamic Fund Ratings* vs the average fund in the sector
- **£45,920 EXTRA** return, on average, after 5 years – from £100,000 initial investment
- **92.16% likelihood** of outperformance – *Dynamic Fund Selection* outperformed in 188/204 five year periods

We are not aware of any other fund rating system that can demonstrate added value on this scale. *[We make the complete evidence publicly available on the FundExpert.co.uk web site, fund sector by fund sector[40]].*

Why "*Dynamic*"?

Using the UK stock market as an example, there are 41 different sectors which make up the stock market as a whole.

At any one time, some of those sectors will be pushing the UK market higher, while other sectors are static or falling. This is the case in all stock markets around the globe.

Most experienced investors will admit that trying to successfully time getting into the winning sectors and out of the losing sectors is beyond them, or, at best, difficult.

But at any one time a small number of fund managers will have a bigger proportion in those winning sectors, and as a result their fund will be performing noticeably better than the rest. I don't care whether that is because he/she is skillful or lucky – that is irrelevant to me. I just need to know that right now this is what we might call a winning fund, a fund with momentum.

This winning streak for a fund, the period when momentum is maintained, tends to run for 6-12 months. We know this because we crunched the numbers for all funds across all sectors and tested a range of periods. It is also confirmed by a raft of authoritative research stretching back decades (albeit primarily regarding individual shares).[41]

Sleight of hand?

The evidence in the table above is so stark, and the process so straightforward, that I feel some might sense a sleight-of-hand.

I have often asked the question of myself, **"Why oh why has no one done this before?"**.

The truth is that this is nothing new. The first research identifying the success of a Momentum approach to selecting investments was back in the 1930s, and there are now hundreds if not thousands of research papers available via a simple Google search.[42] Many billions of pounds is invested around the world using this technique, by large institutions and hedge funds, what you might call "the smart money".

But this has never previously been brought to the attention of retail investors (that's you) as a straightforward means of selecting *funds*.

Why did this not happen earlier?

I think there has been complacency in the financial services industry, and particularly in the field of investment funds (both fund managers and advisers).

In addition, the investing public has not been sufficiently demanding – partly this has arisen because it has never been made sufficiently clear that there are vastly better alternatives. I hope that we have now changed that.

If you get this right, this scale of extra growth will be life-changing for many long-term investors.

NEXT STEPS

I will return to precisely how you can use ***Dynamic Fund Ratings*** in a later chapter. But first we must all understand what can go wrong and be prepared.

14. The Worst Time Ever

Having read about Harry's very happy experience, you might now be feeling fearless, and puffing out your chest. But take care, it isn't always as easy, as I will explore later.

For now, let's explore if Harry was just lucky. I know we saw that Harry went through some hair-raising downs as well as ups. But the cynic in you needs more evidence.

The problem with too many investment approaches is that they are profitable only with the benefit of hindsight, and the luck of timing, and aren't repeatable.

So, let's check how Harry would have done if he had begun investing at the **worst time ever** – **January 2000**.

A very bad time to invest

January 2000 was the top of an extraordinary bull market, on some measures the most extreme in 300-odd years. But the bubble was about to burst, tipping us into a multi-year bear market.

Let's assume you began investing using Harry's process in January 2000. His means for selecting funds is now encapsulated in our ***Dynamic Fund Ratings***, and I'm assuming you used these ratings in 2000 to select UK growth funds from the popular "UK All Companies" fund sector. It works like this:

- Buy the 3 top rated UK growth funds using *Dynamic Fund Ratings.*
- Sell these 6 months later,
- and then buy the 3 top-rated funds of the most recent 6 months.
- Repeat this every 6 months.

If you stuck to your process to select funds and applied it with discipline from January 2000 to December 2016 this is what your success looked like:

Chart 4: The performance of the Dynamic Fund Portfolio vs. an index tracking fund (Jan 2000-Dec 2016)

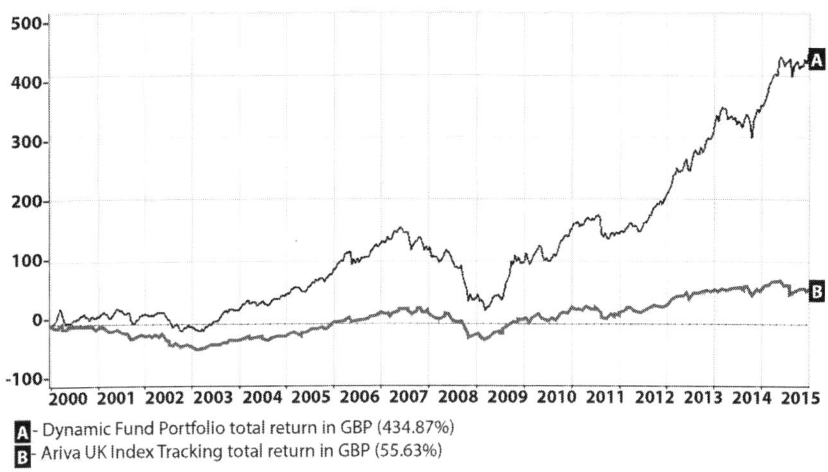

Even if you started investing at such a terrible time, sticking to your process meant you massively outperformed the market as a whole (represented by the badly lagging index tracker) and the average UK growth fund.

To give those returns some context, here is the chart broken-down assuming an initial investment of £100,000. The third column illustrates how much you *lost* by not having a winning process to select funds, that is by investing into an index tracker or the average UK growth fund:

	Invested on 01/01/2000	Value as at 31/12/2016	Your loss vs. Dynamic Portfolio
Dynamic Portfolio	£100,000	£510,860	
Index Tracking Fund	£100,000	£179,950	**You lost** £330,910
Average UK Growth Fund	£100,000	£200,710	**You lost** £310,150

NEXT STEPS

I know from our live webinars that at this point some of you will be champing at the bit, ready to throw some money at the practical ideas presented so far.

But there will also be some of you still lacking a little in confidence.

If you are in the latter camp, let's explore how you can better the results of:

1. Arguably the greatest investor of all time, **Warren Buffett** (AKA the Sage of Omaha).
2. The most prominent fund manager in the UK today, **Neil Woodford.**

I'll start with Warren Buffett.

15. You Can Do Better Than Buffett – The Evidence

Warren Buffett is a remarkable human being. No, he is more than remarkable. He is unique. And he is worth $66.8 billion.

Yet, you can now do much better than Buffett! The evidence is clear.

My colleagues and I have said it many times, and it can never be repeated too often. There are two key ingredients for long-term investing success.

Discipline and process.

Process is primarily about how you select investments (though also about when you sell).

But *which* **process?** One approach to process is to model yourself on a person or process where there is clear and irrefutable evidence of success. Don't try and reinvent the wheel if someone else has already done it – however galling you might find that as a rugged individualist.

Even those who believe that you and I cannot consistently outperform the market must accept the volume of evidence highlighting exceptional individuals. Warren Buffet is one such individual.

Warren Buffett is lauded as a *Value* investor and it is often said in the media that if you wish to model success you should mimic Buffett – and why not, because this guy has grown his fortune to $66.8 billion. Sadly, **for the vast majority of investors, this is nonsense**.

Buffett is an extraordinary man, with an intellect and mindset and discipline which frankly none of us can hope to mimic. If it was possible, there would be obviously successful mini-Buffetts scattered around the world – but there aren't.

The point is that you can only mimic what is practical and realistic for you. *Value* investing is simply not practicable for most private investors:

> *"Value investing requires a great deal of hard work, unusually strict discipline, and a long-term investment horizon. Few are willing and able to devote sufficient time and effort to become value investors, and only a fraction of those have the proper mind-set to succeed"*

That's from none other than the high priest of Value investing, Seth Klarman[43].

The investing process that is right for *you* must have the following ingredients:

- clear and understandable
- repeatable with relative ease
- evidence of success over a long period

I have already illustrated on numerous occasions how using a **Momentum** process to select funds meets all these criteria, AKA our ***Dynamic Fund Ratings.***

Let's see how this approach has shaped up in recent years versus Warren Buffett's vehicle, Berkshire Hathaway.

So that currency moves don't skew the figures, the Berkshire Hathaway numbers are for a U.S.-based investor versus the U.S. stock market, and the *Dynamic Fund Portfolio* results are for a UK-based investor versus the UK stock market.

Over the five years to end 2015, we used these ***Dynamic Fund Ratings*** to select UK growth funds, exactly as you saw earlier:

- Buy the 3 top rated UK growth funds using *Dynamic Fund Ratings.*
- Sell these 6 months later.
- And then buy the 3 top-rated funds of the most recent 6 months.

- Repeat this every 6 months.

The gain was 113% using this process over the 5 years *(outperforming the UK stock market by a huge 100%).*

In contrast, Berkshire Hathaway (the Buffett vehicle for *Value* investing) was up just 64%, and only 4% better than the U.S. stock market.

It is the extra growth compared to the index which is the most impressive feature of funds selected by using ***Dynamic Fund Ratings***.

	5 years	
	%	Index %
Berkshire Hathaway (USD)	64.21%	60.70%
Dynamic Fund Portfolio (GBP)	113.25%	12.45%

To summarise, you must focus on an investment process that is practical for you, apply it over years with *discipline*, and your success should be assured. [44]

And don't get caught in the headlights of the apparent investment stars...

...because on further examination they just might not be so hot.

Anticipating "angry from Ambridge" letters at my effrontery to suggest you can do better than Warren Buffett, let me clarify a point here. You can't do what Buffett can do, and you certainly can't do better than him by doing what he does.

But you can do something different and improve on the performance which he can achieve today. That "something different" is something which *is* achievable by you, and, more to the point, is something which Warren Buffett can *not* do. And this goes to the heart of why you can do better You have the flexibility which a multi-billionaire does not .

He is just too big an investor to nimbly exploit the opportunities presented by something like ***Dynamic Fund Ratings***.

You can exploit processes to select investments which a multi-billionaire cannot.

So, hold back on that angry letter or email! Warren Buffett is an extraordinary man and investor. You just need to exploit your strengths (which are his weaknesses).

16. You Can Beat Neil Woodford Too – The Evidence

If you have rushed to this chapter and skipped the last, can I ask you to quickly go back and read the last three paragraphs of the prior chapter.

Done that? Thank you.

You can do this. You can beat Neil Woodford.

It is the same basic principles as you saw earlier:

- have a clear and proven process for selecting outstanding funds.
- apply that process consistently.

Then you have the tools to outperform Neil Woodford.

Let's take a look at the evidence.

Neil Woodford is hugely successful as a fund manager. His career dates back to his earlier years at Invesco Perpetual managing the Income and High Income funds before he left to set up his own shop in March 2014.

His Invesco Perpetual Income fund grew **864%** from January 1995 to March 2014.

Over that same period, a portfolio of UK growth funds selected by using our ***Dynamic Fund Ratings*** would have grown **1197%**.

That's a difference of **333%**,[45] which is pretty substantial extra growth for our ratings method versus a fund manager of such stature.

Neil Woodford's approach to selecting stocks is obviously successful, and how he built his success is fascinating. When he announced he was leaving Invesco Perpetual I said:

> ***"Neil Woodford's success over the last 15 years has to a large extent been based on one huge bet****, what we have called the biggest and longest bet in fund management history – a consistently large overweight in defensives, in particular utilities, tobacco, and pharmaceuticals. Would any other manager have had the foresight to begin this strategy? And the fortitude to continue with it over such a prolonged period?" (Fundexpert.co.uk blog 15/10/13)*

Was he lucky? Fortunate in his timing? Or was he skillful in a way which most of his peers weren't? Do we care? Should we care?

Think about it. Investors using our ***Dynamic Fund Ratings*** don't care if the manager of the fund which they buy is lucky or skillful – that is not something to which they have to commit any thinking time. This investor simply invests into whichever fund has momentum in any six-month period, as indicated by ***Dynamic Fund Ratings***.

You can see from chart 5 below, the Dynamic portfolio is fairly consistently above Neil's fund the great majority of the time.

Chart 5: The performance of the Dynamic Fund Portfolio vs. Invesco Perpetual Income (Jan 1995-Mar 2014)

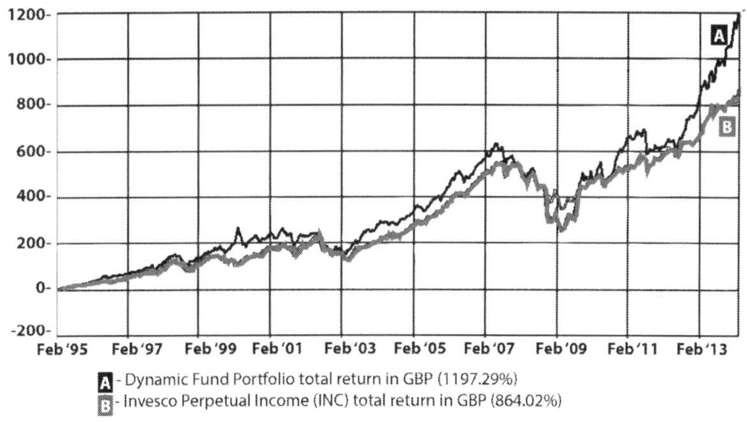

17. More Than One Way to Skin the Fund Managers

Harry's method of investing in funds illustrates one route to achieve outstanding investment results. But you will recall from chapter 6 that **Momentum** was just one of the four proven and well established alternatives to simply investing into index trackers.

In this chapter, I want to give you the most recent numbers for each of these different approaches if you had taken advantage of them via funds.

Remember, in each case you simply use ordinary mainstream funds to achieve extraordinary results.

To recap, the Efficient Market Hypothesis says that you (and by extension the fund managers) shouldn't be able to consistently perform better than the stock market index – and if this was a true reflection of the real world, the best option would be to invest in a fund which mirrors that index – a so-called index tracking fund, a fund which requires no active input from a fund manager.

This theory does not stand up to scrutiny, and I have provided evidence to illustrate that throughout this book, in particular highlighting four proven strategies:

1. Momentum investing
2. Value investing
3. Small cap investing
4. High Yield investing

Detailed definitions on each of these were set out in chapter 6. Now I want to broaden out this evidence, and introduce you to some new ideas which would work for you.

In each case below we assume that you started investing in January 2000, so there could not be a tougher test.

Remember four things:

- This test is from January 2000, an appallingly bad time to start investing as we saw in chapter 14.
- These are straightforward approaches, easy to apply by private investors or their advisers.
- You are buying mainstream funds.
- The key with each of these approaches is that they force you to make better choices from amongst the huge volume of mainstream funds.

The Evidence – Extraordinary Extra Growth For YOU

In each table below, we not only show the extra percentage growth, but also, to bring this to life, we show you this extra growth in cash terms assuming you invested £100,000 in January 2000.

1. **Momentum investing** simply means buying winners, using the process discovered by Harry and set out in chapter 11: i.e. buying the three funds from your chosen sector with the highest ***Dynamic Fund Ratings*** (in that case from the UK All Companies sector), and repeating this every 6 months.

The table below clearly shows the extraordinary extra growth, cash in your pocket, if you used our ***Dynamic Fund Ratings*** to select funds – ***an extra £310,150***.

Momentum strategy	Total Return	Extra growth on £100,000 investment
Momentum	410.86%	£310,150 EXTRA GROWTH
UK All Companies Sector Avg.	100.71%	
FTSE 100	85.43%	

2. **Value investing**, you will recall, isn't simply buying what is cheap – a company might have a low share price for very good reasons. Rather, it is buying what is cheap *without* good reason. So rather than buying a winner (Momentum investing) you are buying a certain type of loser.

There is no “Value” fund sector, so in this case we have chosen the **Schroder Recovery** fund as their flagship Value fund, and because Schroders are the most outspoken Value proponents in the UK.

As I have handpicked a fund, this example is not one which can be systematically replicated going forward. Nonetheless, it adequately highlights another exception to the idea that markets are efficient and that you should only buy index trackers.

In this case, you generated ***£362,700 extra growth.***

Value strategy	Total Return	Extra growth on £100,000 investment
Schroder Recovery	463.41%	£362,700 EXTRA GROWTH
UK All Companies Sector Avg.	100.71%	
FTSE 100	85.43%	

3. **Small cap investing** is, obviously, buying smaller companies or funds which invest into smaller companies. In this example I show how:

1. Even the average UK smaller companies fund outperformed the wider market.
2. In addition (and this is the really interesting bit), I show how this would be vastly better if you use ***Dynamic Fund Ratings*** to identify the small cap funds with greatest potential every 6 months.

As you can see in the table below, by combining small cap investing with our ***Dynamic Fund Ratings*** (a form of Momentum), you achieve the best outcome in this chapter's examples – ***an extra £490,500!***

Small Cap momentum strategy	Total Return	Extra growth on £100,000 investment
Momentum + Small Cap	682.38%	£490,500 EXTRA GROWTH
UK Smaller Cos. Sector Avg.	191.88%	
FTSE 100	85.43%	

4. High Yield investing means buying shares with above-average dividend yields and reinvesting these – funds in the UK Equity Income fund sector do just that.

As you can see in the table below, just the average UK Equity Income fund provided a decent chunk of extra growth compared to the index.

You can do even better by combining high yield investing with our ***Dynamic Fund Ratings*** (a form of Momentum)– ***an extra £50,400***.

High Yield strategy	Total Return	Extra growth on £100,000 investment
Momentum + High Yield	185.12%	£50,400 EXTRA GROWTH
UK Equity Income Sector Avg.	134.72%	
FTSE 100	85.43%	

It should be clear to you now that these approaches to investing, enabling you to identify funds with outstanding potential, are no theory – this is what actually happens and these strategies are all possible for private investors like you, or your advisers. They just require a little concentrated effort on a regular basis – perhaps **no more than 30 minutes every 6 months**.

Though most professionals underperform the market, as you have seen, private investors like you have a fantastic edge; no-one is more excited by the potential for your money than you!

Now you can visualise that your rewards can be extraordinary and life-changing.

NEXT STEPS

If you have already been tempted to check out what others have to say on issues such as Momentum, you might have read of certain weaknesses to this approach. I want to make sure you understand the wrinkles you will encounter along the way, so that you are properly prepared.

I will make sure we explore them thoroughly and identify solutions that will work for you.

18. What Can Go Wrong

Nothing is perfect.

No approach to investing is perfect.

Nor is any single way to select funds.

I have shown you some impressive results if you adopt a straightforward and proven process for selecting funds. But we must not be complacent, and work to understand:

- What might go wrong.
- What you can do about this.

I have read volumes about **Momentum** investing – the research stretches back decades, starting in the 1930s [46]. And uniquely, I have been crunching the numbers in the context of funds since we first launched our *TopFunds Guide* in 2002. So, I have built a decent knowledge on this issue on top of 30 years of experience, both advising, writing and researching.

The national press cover this issue from time to time and they very kindly tend to get in touch. They also ask the view of others, and this is where it gets interesting. While very experienced in years, my peers have typically not crunched the numbers as I have, nor ever used **Momentum** as a tool for selecting funds for clients.

When these other pundits are asked "what are the problems with **Momentum** investing?" they tend to repeat what someone else said, who also hadn't crunched the numbers.

So, let's explore the two oft-mentioned problems and see if they hold water.

1. It is claimed that **Momentum** fails at turning points for markets.
2. It is claimed that **Momentum** is more risky.

1. Does Momentum fail at turning points for markets?

To recap, you buy a fund today because it was the top performer of its kind in the last 6 months – 6 months later you repeat this process, selling the current holding and buying the latest top performer – this is the process built into our ***Dynamic Fund Ratings***.

Now suppose that you bought this fund one month before the stock market went into a tailspin. You might expect that the funds that had led the performance tables in the prior 6 months will now lead the market lower, losing more than most of their peers.

So, let's explore that at the time of the market collapse from January 2000 (as the tech bubble burst) and from September 2008 (when Lehman Brothers went bust and took the world to the brink of Great Depression II).

Turning Point 1: The bursting of the tech bubble

January 2000. This was the top of an extraordinary bull market, on some measure the most extreme in 300-odd years. The bubble was about to burst, tipping us into an ugly bear market of three years' duration.

Using our ***Dynamic Fund Ratings*** to select UK growth funds, in January 2000 you would have invested into these three funds:

- Artemis Capital
- Artemis UK Select
- AXA-Framlington UK Select Opportunities

In July 2000, you would have switched out of those funds into the latest top-rated funds, and so on, every 6 months.

In the table below, we show the performance of this *Dynamic Fund Portfolio* compared with the FTSE 100 (representing the UK stock market) and the average UK growth fund (i.e. populating the UK All Companies fund sector).

By the end of the first 6 months (June 2000), our portfolio was *up* 6.86% compared to *down* 7.87% for the index, a difference of 14.73% in just 6 months.

So clearly, no underperformance of our Momentum-style portfolio at the turning point from bull market to bear, as some have suggested there should have been.

Table 1: Dynamic Fund Portfolio (DFP) vs FTSE 100 and UK All Co's sector (2000-2005)

	2000		2001		2002	
	Jan-Jun	July-Dec	Jan-Jun	July-Dec	Jan-Jun	July-Dec
Dynamic Fund Portfolio (DFP)	6.86	4.93	8.00	-4.74	-6.51	-12.32
FTSE 100	-7.87	-0.39	-8.11	-6.51	-9.33	-14.70
UK All Cos. sector avg.	-3.70	-0.40	-7.78	-6.90	-9.90	-15.58
DFP vs. Index	*+14.73*	*+5.32*	*+16.11*	*+1.77*	*+2.82*	*+2.38*
DFP vs. sector avg.	*+10.56*	*+5.33*	*+15.78*	*+2.16*	*+3.39*	*+3.26*

	2003		2004		2005	
	Jan-Jun	July-Dec	Jan-Jun	July-Dec	Jan-Jun	July-Dec
Dynamic Fund Portfolio	9.61	20.99	9.90	8.26	8.98	14.73
FTSE 100	4.54	14.69	1.66	10.41	8.33	10.46
UK All Cos. sector avg.	8.16	13.80	3.88	8.73	7.24	12.22
DFP vs. Index	+5.07	+6.3	+8.24	-2.15	+0.65	+4.27
DFP vs. sector avg.	+1.45	+7.19	+6.02	-0.47	+1.74	+2.51

The news gets even better.

If you look at the table above, in all but one period (July-Dec 2004) our *Dynamic Fund Portfolio* outperforms the stock market index and the sector average. And in that period the portfolio is still positive, it just doesn't rise as much as the other two.

That is a superb testimony to the Momentum strategy during this period.

You can see this progress in the chart.

Chart 6: Dynamic Fund Portfolio vs FTSE 100

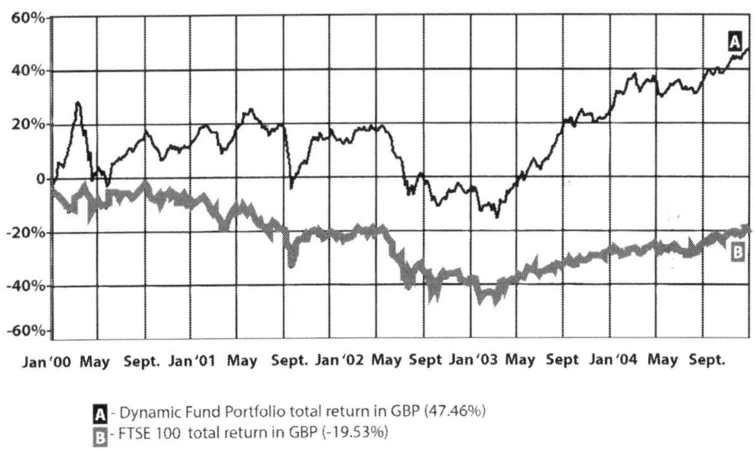

Turning point 2: Lehman Brothers bust in 2008

More recently, the failure of Lehman Brothers. in September 2008 triggered sharp falls across the globe.

If you had begun investing into the UK stock market in January 2008 using our ***Dynamic Fund Ratings***, you would have invested into three funds:

- JOHCM UK Opportunities
- Newton UK Equity
- Threadneedle UK Extended Alpha

In July 2008, you would have switched out of those funds, as you now know, choosing the latest top funds using our ***Dynamic Fund Ratings***. And so on, every 6 months.

In the table below, for each discrete six-month period, we show the performance of the Momentum-style *Dynamic Fund Portfolio* compared with the UK stock market and the average UK growth fund (which populates the UK All Companies sector).

For example, at the end of the first six-month period, June 2008, the *Dynamic Fund Portfolio* was down 8.56%, whereas the index was worse, down 10.82%.

Table 2: Dynamic Fund Portfolio vs FTSE 100 and UK All Co's sector (2008-2010)

	2008		2009		2010	
	Jan-Jun	July-Dec	Jan-Jun	July-Dec	Jan-Jun	July-Dec
Dynamic Fund Portfolio (DFP)	-8.56	-27.94	-0.05	39.31	-3.26	31.34
FTSE 100	-10.82	-17.49	-1.61	26.63	-7.39	24.42
UK All Cos. sector avg.	-11.22	-22.85	4.54	24.49	-4.13	23.78
DFP vs. Index	*+2.26*	*-10.45*	*+1.56*	*+12.68*	*+4.13*	*+6.92*
DFP vs. sector avg.	*+2.66*	*-5.09*	*-4.59*	*+14.82*	*+0.87*	*+7.56*

Our Momentum-style portfolio fell more than the index in the next 6 months, was marginally better in the first half of 2009, and was outstanding from then on versus the index and the average UK growth fund.

So that forensic look at each six-month period doesn't reveal any great weakness with Momentum.

But perhaps we're missing something, so let's look at this another way.

The low for the UK stock market was March 2009. From January 2008 to that low, the Momentum portfolio fell by 46%. That compares to a fall of 42% by the FTSE 100 over the same period. A small difference, certainly not worrying.

Looking at the chart below, you can see that our *Dynamic Fund Portfolio* (black line) returned to positive territory in September 2010 compared to the starting point of January 2008, and it went into positive territory two months faster than the FTSE 100.

Chart 7: Our Dvnamic Fund Portfolio vs FTSE 100

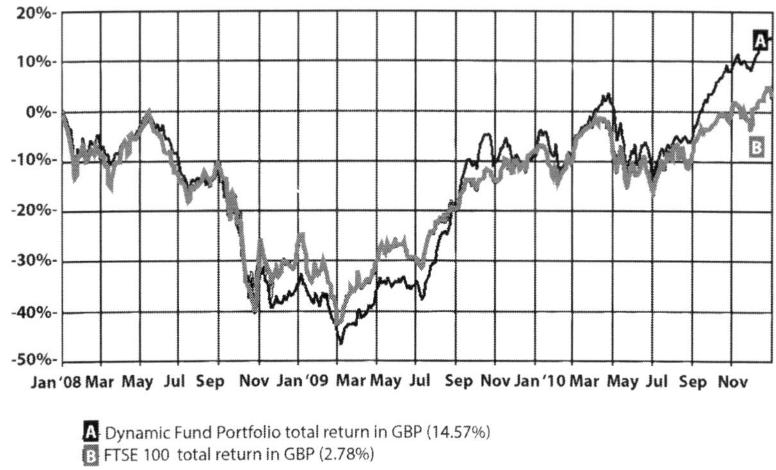

2. Is Momentum more risky?

For an investor in funds, risk means volatility, in other words how much a fund goes up and down. If it is more risky, it will go up and down more than its peers.

We considered this to some extent with the last two examples of turning points – when we saw nothing worrying that would stop you from exploiting a Momentum-style process for selecting funds versus buying an index tracker.

There are a number of other measures to judge the riskiness or volatility of any investment approach.

Table 3: Dynamic Fund Portfolio vs FTSE 100 and UK growth sector (1994-2015)

	Performance		Monthly			
	Overall (%)	Annu-alised (%)	Historic VaR	Max Gain	Max Loss	Negative months
Dynamic Fund Portfolio	1410.6	13.46	4.12	15.83	*-15.49*	86
FTSE 100	345.47	7.58	6.33	9.09	*-12.86*	101
UK All Companies Sector Avg	329.15	7.01	5.03	12.28	*-15.45*	94

The above table shows a number of statistics that enable you to compare our *Dynamic Fund Portfolio*[47] with both the UK stock market index and the average UK growth fund.

For instance:

The Momentum-style Dynamic Fund Portfolio had fewer *negative months* than either the index or the average UK growth fund.

The *maximum monthly loss* was slightly higher at -15.49% for the Momentum-style portfolio versus the index and the average UK growth fund.

However, that is more than compensated for by the *maximum monthly gain*, which was 15.83% for *Dynamic Fund Portfolio* vs. 9.09% for the index.

The VaR is "Monthly Value at Risk", a more technical measure. The VaR figure for the average UK growth fund is 5.03%. This means that in 19 of those months out of 20 you should not, on average, expect a fall in the value of more than 5.03% in one month. In the 20th month the loss might be more severe (October 1987 being an extreme example, with a 20%+ fall in one month).

For the *Dynamic Fund Portfolio,* the monthly risk of 4.12% is less than that of both the average growth fund (5.03%) and the index (6.06%).

It is clear from all of the above that there is no evidence that a Momentum-style process for selecting funds is more risky than alternatives, on the contrary. Those "experts" who trot out these supposed drawbacks simply haven't done their homework – at least not with funds.

Next Steps

Nonetheless, there are other risk issues you should take more seriously when thinking about your approach to investing generally, and selecting funds in particular – and these apply whatever your approach, even if you only buy index trackers, and even more so if you buy individual shares.

Sometimes bad things happen, worse than 2000 and 2008.

The Japan Problem.

19. The Japan Problem

Now I want to focus on what can REALLY go wrong.

This isn't a problem for someone selecting funds based on a **Momentum** process.

It is a problem for *all* investors, in all types of investments, however you select those investments.

Bad things happen. And it can happen worse than 2000 and 2008 (which, by the way, we have just observed weren't so bad after all if you used our *Dynamic Fund Ratings* to select funds).

For the sake of argument, here are three categories of falls in stock markets.[48]

1. **A correction** is typically in the range of 10-20%. It will generate twitchy headlines, and might unnerve you a tad, but you just need to be patient and it will be gone as quickly as it arrived.
2. **A bear market**. You will encounter falls in the range of 20-50%. Yes, it can be scary. Though there

were three since 2000 and patience and steady nerves or a good adviser got you through them.

3. **A secular bear market**, a multi-year downturn which lasts more than a couple of years. You should expect falls in excess of 50%. We call this "**The Japan Problem**".

The Japan Problem, and how you can sidestep it, is our focus in this chapter.

First allow me to go back a stage. The good news is that if you buy a UK stock market fund you are effectively buying 50-100 different underlying companies. This means you have eliminated the risk of losing all your money because just one company goes bust – and you have a professional fund manager crawling all over each of these companies to limit the risk of even ONE going bust. This is a nod to the original idea of Van Ketwich in 1774.

Plus, you can easily factor into your thinking occasional years of weakness as described in the first two categories above. These can be dealt with by patience and a sensible timeframe for investment (and the sort of plan we will set out for you later on).

But very occasionally, perhaps once every few decades, it can get somewhat worse.

In real terms (that is after allowing for inflation) the U.S. stock market peak of 1929 was not regained until 1954 (25 years). We call periods like this "accidents of history" – what Nassim Taleb has more recently called "black swans".[49] If our parents or grandparents had invested early in the last century, could they really have guessed that their lives would be consumed by two World Wars, the Wall Street Crash, and the Great Depression?

Sometimes fate is just going to deal you a tough hand. Very rare, but you cannot ignore this possibility in your planning.

Supposing that the whole UK economy went downhill rapidly for some reason? And stayed down for a prolonged period?

One single huge downturn spanning many years? There isn't a VERY severe example on this scale in the UK, so let me present you with Japan, at worst down a huge 80% from the peak in 1989, and still down 51%[50].

Chart 8: Japanese Stock Market from 1990-2015

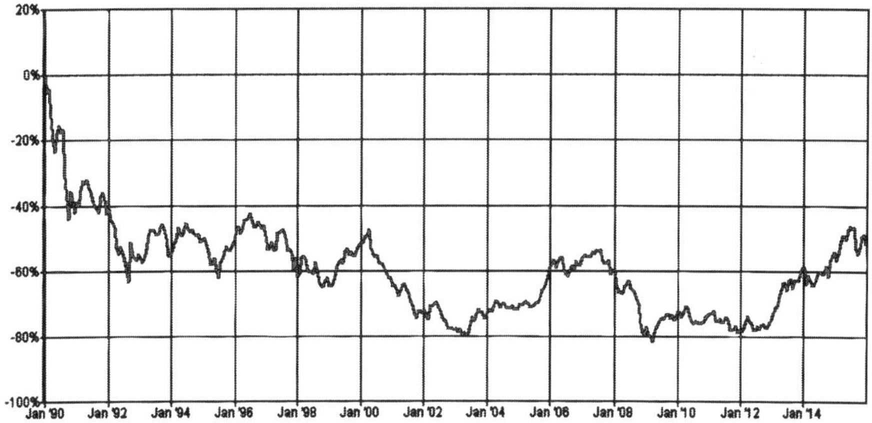

Nikkei 226 price-only in JPY [-51.09%]

Here is a chart of the Japanese stock market from 1990 to 2015 – it has been substantially down for 25 years! If you were Japanese and managing your own portfolio or SIPP in the late 1980s, you would very probably have had most of your money in your home market – clinging to the home market is what most investors do, including in the UK and US.

Could such a prolonged collapse happen here? Of course it could. And don't think you (or I) are so clever that:

1. You will see it coming.

2. You will do something about it in good time.

And don't think it couldn't happen here because that was "merely" Japan. Japan is still the world's third-biggest economy and their insights and sophistication are every bit as great as in the UK or U.S. or Europe.

How could you have sidestepped the problems of Japan at an early stage? In two ways:

1. A certain kind of diversification.

2. A stop loss.

Diversification is a great tool for limiting risk in your portfolio; it is shorthand for not having all your eggs in one basket. It is what Van Ketwich brought to investors with the first fund in 1774, and what Markovitz took to a new level in 1952 with the idea of an Efficient Portfolio.

The theory of diversification is that some of your assets will move up while others fall – so your portfolio as a whole does not take a huge hit from being over-concentrated in one area.

As we do not know from where next year's winner might spring, you should hold a spread of types of funds and asset classes so that, on average, you will get a positive return. In practice, this can get quite complicated, but that's the theory of diversification.

The risks of **not** diversifying are very clear in the real world. While it might seem strange that anyone would have most or all of their wealth in the shares of one company, it has been more common than you might think, and with ugly consequences.

For example, many bank branch workers in Lloyds built substantial values in Lloyds Bank shares through options built up over their working lives – but plans for retirement or second homes or a healthy bonus income were destroyed as the value of their shares fell over 95% from the peak at the turn of the millennium.

It was similar for employees of the giant company Enron in the U.S. – very unsophisticated employees, as well as highly paid senior management, had huge wealth wiped out when the company was exposed as an extraordinary fraud, unbeknownst to those employees. Not only were the shares worthless, but pension promises were also worthless.

Even with a fund, despite its inherent diversification across 50-100 different companies, you can

get caught out. Those domestic Japanese investors would have had life savings decimated in the years following the 1989 peak. If the WHOLE market is trashed, it doesn't provide any protection if all the underlying investments are invested into that one market.

That's the BAD news.

Dynamic Diversification

The good news is that you can automatically and dynamically adjust your exposure away from a failing asset classes (like Japan in the latter example).

For example, suppose that in December 1989 you were 100% invested into Japan. Once Japan started to fall away, if you used a certain Momentum-style strategy, you would only have been invested for a short period (6 months) after the peak – in that case the fall would have been restricted to about 20% - with 20-plus future years to make up that lost ground.

This significant risk-reduction rule is built into our *50/50 Portfolio*, and I will look at this in more detail in chapter 22 – in a nutshell it ensures you don't encounter *The Japan Problem.*

As you will see, this is a highly effective way to ensure you do not remain invested in asset classes which keep heading south for years.

Nonetheless, you can do even better in terms of risk reduction.

Stop losses

A stop-loss means that you decide you will sell your fund if it falls by a certain amount – so you literally stop the loss from getting any bigger.

While diversification is an important tool, particularly *Dynamic Diversification*, you should not be over-reliant on it. The problem with diversification is that during the worst periods for markets nearly ALL asset classes, all around the globe, can fall sharply – this was the lesson of 2008.

This is the one big limitation of diversification – be aware of this. Events like *The Japan Problem* are certainly not commonplace. But events like these only need to occur once in your lifetime to destroy your lifetime plans and ambitions.

This is not an excuse NOT to diversify – it is merely a warning that you really need more than just diversification to limit your risks.

And stop-losses add that significant other string to your bow.

Let's take another example to give stop-losses a little context.

The U.S. stock market looked over-valued in December 1996 when Alan Greenspan (heading up the Federal Reserve) famously saw "irrational exuberance". This put many people off investing into the U.S. (yes, me included).

But there is a problem – a stock market can remain over-valued, and keep going up, for years before it finally peaks. And that is exactly what happened.

Over the following 4 years the U.S. stock market went up in excess of 80%!

Stock market valuations are far from fine-tuning tools, and can be a very costly distraction. The knowledge that you have stop-losses can give you the confidence to invest, and stay invested, despite apparent over-valuation – you don't become obsessed with, and distracted by, valuations.

There are two issues for you to decide in respect of your stop-loss:

1. At what level should you sell: e.g. when it drops 5% or 10%?
2. And when should you buy back in?

We have researched this in great detail, and crunched these numbers back to 1985, testing a number of permutations.

There is no perfect answer, but, in a nutshell, the most effective stop-loss method was selling on a 10% fall.

Selling with a 5% fall continually whip-saws you in an out of markets – this is costly and not recommended.

In our advanced courses and on FundExpert.co.uk, I look at this in more detail, including when you buy back into funds, and which funds. For now, you should note three issues:

- Stop-losses on funds cannot be automated. You will need to use a service which will send you an alert when the price falls 10%, unless you are doing daily monitoring yourself, which is impractical for most people
- When you receive such an alert, telling you the value has fallen 10%, you still have to action it. This is obvious, but many people still struggle with inertia once funds are purchased – your plan is too easily sidestepped.
- Acting on a stop-loss is not necessarily easy. Psychologists have shown that realising a loss is mentally painful – so most of us try to avoid this pain and do nothing.

A stop-loss is a powerful tool to prevent the potential for extreme damage to your portfolio – but applying it requires some discipline. As such there is great value in a third party service which will prod you into action – more on that later.

NEXT STEPS

I want to digress now, and make sure we are all agreed on some key terminology which is bandied around.

20. Your Investment Journey – Risk of Confusion

Talking of what can go wrong, misunderstanding can and does arise because our industry bandies words around which are poorly understood within the industry let alone further afield.

"Risk" is such a word.

Please don't turn the page! This really does need to be addressed, and it is a key consideration in the plan which we will be building together shortly.

> *"The value of your investments can go down as well as up."*

On the one hand, this is a vital bit of small print to which more attention should be paid. On the other hand, as vital as it is, and as straightforward as it seems, it is confusing.

The regulators call this the *"Risk warning"*, and it has been parroted for decades.

Yet strictly speaking, it is not a warning about **risk** as most people might understand the term – it is a warning about **volatility**.

What is the difference?

Most people would think of risk as the possibility of a loss, either partial or total.

For example, if you invested £100,000 into the shares of one company, the risk of a *total* loss, if the company went bankrupt, is very real.

In contrast, when you buy a fund, the fund might hold 50-100 individual companies. So, a *total* loss is only realistically possible if the earth was hit by another planet. Or if there is fraud by the (heavily regulated) fund management group. Thankfully, there is no precedent for either event.

Therefore, with funds it is a *partial* loss which concerns you: i.e. you sell your fund at a lower price than the price at which you bought it.

This means that, with a fund, a loss can only arise because of *deliberate* action by *you*.

In contrast, **volatility** is simply how much the value of your investments go up and down – your investment journey.

As this book is primarily about funds, and so as not to add to confusion, I will use the terms risk and volatility inter-changeably – for the purposes of this book they mean the same thing.

Therefore, as a fund investor, we can say that risk is about your investment journey.

Have a look at the theoretical charts below. Each fund generated the same growth. But **Fund A** obviously had the more volatile journey. In a choice between the two, and with perfect hindsight, you would obviously choose **Fund B** – a smoother journey, and one less likely to keep you awake at night. This is the theory.

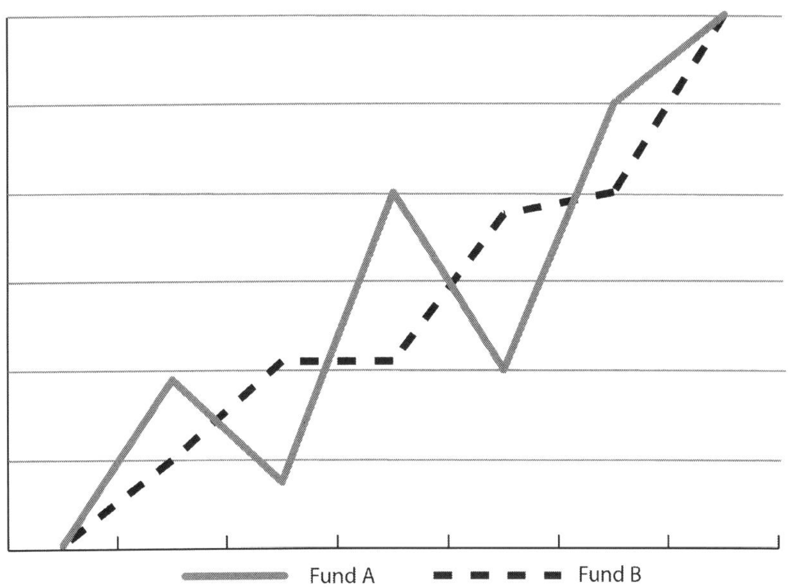

Risk in action

What you might normally expect is reflected in table 1 below, contrasting UK stock market funds with corporate bond funds: i.e. the more risky stock market funds generated somewhat greater returns than lower-risk bond funds. That they were more risky is shown by the maximum monthly loss encountered over the period surveyed.

Table 1: Performance and Maximum Monthly Loss 2010-2015[50]		
Fund Sector	Average Growth %	Max Monthly Loss %
Corporate Bond Funds	28.39	-3.86
UK Stock Market Funds	41.31	-9.25

Table 2 below shows the same idea, but with some additional types of funds, which will interest those of you looking for simpler solutions. The first three rows show three "Mixed" fund sectors.

As the name suggests, funds belonging to the first sector have up to 35% in the stock market.

In the second they can have 20-60% in the stock market, and in the third they can hold 40-85% in the stock market, which should make it the most volatile.

Comparing just these three you can see a perfect illustration of what SHOULD happen in practice. The more risk you take (as illustrated by the column showing the maximum monthly loss), the greater the returns.

To complete the picture, the last row in table 2 below shows the same numbers for UK stock market funds – even more growth, but even more volatility.

Table 2: Performance and Max Monthly Loss 2010-15[52]		
Fund Sector	Average Growth%	Max Monthly Loss %
Mixed Investment 0-35% Shares	17.74	-3.08
Mixed Investment 20-60% Shares	22.06	-3.84
Mixed Investment 40-85% Shares	26.13	-6.19
UK Stock Market Funds	41.31	-9.25

OK. We are now all clear that when we say "risk" it means volatility – it means the price going up and down, the extent to which is shown by the maximum monthly loss in the last two tables.

What level of volatility is acceptable to you? This is important when you decide on the type or types of funds which are appropriate for you.

Imagine you invested £100,000 just 6 months ago. There is some unexpected news, and the stock market, and the value of your fund, falls to £70,000, down 30%.

How would you feel?

- *would it cause you grave concern and worry?*

Or

- would you be relatively relaxed?

Even if relatively well off, with secure income, such falls may still give you sleepless nights – how you might react is a very personal matter.

You need to make a hard-nosed decision about whether you can cope with these sorts of ups and downs.

The stock markets can and do play games with your mind, in particular with the powerful emotions of fear and greed. (Which is another reason to apply a stop-loss, as set out in chapter 19.)

You must try to avoid being panicked into selling, and realising a loss unnecessarily – a plan put together in less stressful times is key to this, **call it pre-commitment**.

Lots of choices beyond the stock market

In the above, I have considered falls in the stock market. Throughout the book, I mostly use stock market funds as examples because they are at the centre of most investors' portfolios.

But you have many choices beyond the stock market. In table 2 above, I gave you a feel for the three "Mixed" sectors. For those who want to keep it very simple, there is probably a fund in one of these sectors for everyone. If you want to limit your stock market exposure, have a look at *Mixed 0-35%,* for example.

The UK growth funds (UK All Companies sector) had a maximum fall of 9% in the period reviewed. In contrast, the average fund in the *Mixed 0-35%* sector encountered a fall no greater than 3% - perhaps you would find that less scary?

That's food for thought, to which I will return in chapter 22.

NEXT STEPS

After 20 chapters, we have not mentioned what, for many people, is the elephant in the room – that's next.

21. Charges, Charges, Charges

The media has an obsession with the charges involved when buying funds.

Not too long ago, I was on the long-running and highly respected Radio 4 Money Box Live programme. Off-air, I and the presenters and other contributors got to the subject of charges. Not charges on funds. But rather charges on the platforms where you purchase the funds, such as FundsNetwork or Hargreaves Lansdown.

It was said that the first thing investors should do, before buying funds, is choose a platform with the lowest charges. The others nodded sagely. I was writing an ebook at the time and it stuck in my head that, at best, this was about the 7th thing you do, certainly not the first.

How you choose funds is many multiples more important than the platform you choose.

I said exactly that (off air) and was asked "what are the other things?" and I reeled them off, to bemused reactions. Not to be put off, I still try and get this message over because it is life-changing for investors who grasp it – and it is a big motivation for me writing this book.

If you truly want to be clear-thinking about this very serious subject (your money!), start by dealing with the most important question:

How should I choose funds?

Put another way, how can I identify funds today with outstanding potential. If you have read my book to this point, you have seen countless examples of why your fund choices are pivotal to your life ambitions. And, most importantly, you have discovered one fantastic way to select funds (*Dynamic Fund Ratings*), supported by a mountain of evidence illustrating how these can transform your financial future.

So why the obsession with charges in much of the media?

Well the reason goes back decades, when charges truly were awful. Back then, pension and endowment policies might have had charges of 25% EVERY YEAR on contributions in the first few years (if you're of a certain age you may remember) – is it any wonder that the financial services industry developed a bad name?!

It wasn't so bad with funds, but there was often an initial charge of 6%.

To a very large extent, this changed for the better from the late 1990s. (Where there were continuing high charge products, they were largely those sold by banks and direct selling companies – not mentioning any names.)

By the late 1990s, advisers were required to clearly tell you how much they earned. Charges on products were reasonably clear and VASTLY improved. If you wanted to do-it-yourself, there were growing options.

For example, discount brokers sprang up, typically offering no initial charges.

Positive changes.

So why the *continuing* obsession with charges?

This could turn into a rant on my part, but let's just say everyone must accept some blame – the fund groups, the adviser community, the regulators, the media, and, yes, even you!

You will doubtless find someone out there who will try and convince you that they can change your life by reducing the charge on your funds, pensions, ISA or whatever by 0.1% or 0.25% etc., per annum. This is nonsense. All they do is distract you from your priority...

...achieving more growth. Achieving more growth through having a better process to select funds.

Here are a couple of examples.

Everyone is a genius when armed with an Excel spreadsheet. And if you can add two percentages together – WOW.

But a basic command of maths seems to convince some that they can disengage brain.

EXAMPLE 1

Fund B	annual charge 0.82%
Fund C	annual charge 0.17%

Which is the better fund?

EXAMPLE 2

Fund X	up 266% last 10 years (after charges)
Fund Y	up 64% last 10 years (after charges)

Which is the better fund?

In fact, Fund B is the same as Fund X. [53]

The performance figures you observe day after day, whether in newspapers or online are all AFTER charges.

Do I want a fund with small charges and limited performance?

Or a fund with outstanding performance AFTER charges?

Surely, we all want to invest into a fund with outstanding growth potential AFTER charges.

Let's look at this another way.

Do you know the difference between 0.25% and 5.96%?

It may seem obvious.

You might even feel insulted that I have asked the question.

The average fund invested into the UK stock market went up by an annualised 7.26% p.a. between July 1994 and June 2014, AFTER charges.[54]

To bring this cold number to life, if you invested £100,000 into this average fund in July 1994, it would have been worth **£406,150** in June 2014 (remember, after charges)

Now assume that someone had been able to reduce the charges on that fund by 0.25%.

That £100,000 would then have grown to **£411,273** (not £406,150). Whoopee? Or a sense of anti-climax?

In contrast, if that investor had used a straightforward process to select funds with outstanding potential, and in the same sector, that £100,000 would have grown to **£1,197,100**.

Now that's a worthwhile difference.

£790,950 extra.

The latter growth equates to 13.22% per annum, which is 5.96% more, every year, than you would have achieved from the average UK stock market fund.

The choice is pretty stark. Would you rather have:

0.25% less in charges?

or

5.96% more in growth, every year?

An average return, or an **extra £790,950?**

You choose.

NEXT STEPS

We're moving into the home straight of our journey. We need to start to build out your plan, to transform your investing success.

22. Are You a Pig Or a Basket Case?

There are still some questions which we need to address together. Among other crucial issues, you have already discovered a great way to select funds, a process.

But you can only choose funds within a context which additionally takes into account:[54]

- The level of volatility with which you are comfortable.
- How many asset classes you wish to consider.
- The extent to which you want a simple solution.

These factors must all be reflected in your portfolio.

To be clear, a portfolio worthy of the name is a very deliberate selection of investments consistent with all of the above three elements, plus your chosen process to select funds. Unfortunately, what most investors actually have is a random collection of investments – this is at the heart of why most investors struggle, achieving mediocrity at best.

If you build a house without a foundation, it will fall down.

Before building your foundation, step by step, I want to give you a sense of four clients I have frequently encountered - remember they are all focussed on growth, not income. [56] These should help you begin to build a profile of yourself, if you have not done so already.

Which of these brief profiles most resembles you:

1. **Do you largely focus on one area**?

   e.g. more than 80% in the UK stock market.

   Or

2. **Do you like to venture farther afield too?**

   e.g. UK stock market plus more than 20% in overseas stock markets

   Or

3. **Do you spread your funds across a variety of different assets, because you are a tad more cautious?**

   e.g. not just stock markets, but significant amounts (40%+) in other assets such as property and bond funds

   Or

4. **Are you quite cautious but would rather a simpler solution, with fewer funds?**

e.g. no more than a handful of funds, where each fund holds a mixture of assets, including stock markets, bonds, and property.

A key difference between each one of these is the extent to which they wish to spread their investments, that diversification issue again.

Before looking at the above in a bit more detail, I want to introduce you to a co-star in our story, Stanley Druckenmiller. He used to work with George Soros, then went out on his own, and was recently worth over $4 billion. Obviously, you and I are doing something much more conventional than the high-rolling hedge funds which Druckenmiller managed – but we can still learn from his like.

This is one quote of his which I love (only slightly tidied up for sense, and where a "pig" is someone who bets everything on one investment idea):

> *"The first thing I heard when I got in the investment business, was bulls make money, bears make money, and pigs get slaughtered. But I'm here to tell you I was a pig.*
>
> *I think diversification and all the stuff they're teaching at business school today is probably the most misguided concept everywhere.*
>
> *And if you look at all the great investors that are as different as Warren Buffett, Carl Icahn, Ken Langone, they tend to be very, very concentrated."*

First a word of caution – don't do this at home! At least not quite as aggressively as Mr D.

For most of us, diversification certainly does matter – we are often dealing with our life savings, and we don't want to make stupid mistakes. It is simply a matter of *how much* we diversify.

Now let's look at each type of investor highlighted above, and the evidence of a winning formula to suit each one. For the avoidance of doubt, in each case that evidence assumes that you began investing in January 2000 – the worst time ever, and the toughest test for any investment process.

The first category of investor set out above is a "pig investor" – someone concentrated in just one area, gorging on it to expand the analogy.

I have observed that a large proportion of DIY investors on FundExpert.co.uk are inclined to be pig investors, typically focussed on the UK stock market.

Some will tell you this is wrong. But I don't think it is either right or wrong - this is simply about your preference, and how comfortable you are with risk as discussed in chapter 20. If you wish to benefit from the dynamism of the best of UK Plc over the long term, this is a perfectly valid approach. **You just need to be absolutely clear that you are doing this effectively, and don't kid yourself otherwise.**

You will recall that from the earliest funds in the late 18th century, a key advantage of a fund was that you did not have all of your eggs in one basket. Even if you now invest into just one fund focussed on the UK stock market, it will probably hold the shares of 50-80 different companies - that's a good spread, a decent level of diversification across many different types of businesses.

You just need to be confident that you are comfortable with the volatility that you will likely encounter with this approach – the sorts of downs as well as ups which I considered in chapter 20, in particular tables 1 and 2.

For example, assume occasional falls in one year of 30%. How will you respond?

More to the point, if you are a long-time holder of investments, how did you respond when this happened in the past?

If you were a little unnerved, that is perfectly understandable. But if you were (or would be) inclined to panic a little, and sell at a large loss, then concentrating your investments into any stock market (UK or otherwise) is perhaps not for you. There is no shame in that – investing everything into stock markets is certainly not for everyone, and your peace of mind is a key consideration.

And you have a lot of other choices, as I touched on at the end of chapter 20.

Here is a table showing the performance of our UK-only portfolio. Every 6 months, we pick the top-performing funds of the last 6 months from the totality of the three

UK stock market sectors (UK All, UK Equity Income, and UK Smaller companies).

The extra performance from this portfolio is extraordinary.

Table 1: *UK-only Dynamic Portfolio* (2000-2016)

	Total Return	Extra growth on £100,000 investment
Dynamic Portfolio	402.58%	**£301,870 EXTRA GROWTH**
UK All Companies Sector Average	100.71%	
FTSE 100	85.43%	

The second category of investor likes to venture further afield, not just the UK stock market but also more than 20% in overseas stock markets. This also represents a significant number of DIY investors on FundExpert.co.uk.

This does spread your investments even more. But whether this reduces your overall volatility is down to a toss of a coin. Much of the time, major stock markets around the world move in the same direction – this is called positive correlation.

There have been some remarkable exceptions over time. For example, in the 1990s the U.S. market went up 431% while Japan dropped 51%. But don't bank on something like this working in your favour.

This approach is more about increasing opportunities for growth than reducing volatility – you are improving the *up* potential but not reducing the *downs*.

We call this the ***50/50 Dynamic Portfolio.*** Every 6 months, we pick the top-performing funds of the last 6 months from the totality of the main non-UK stock market sectors (Europe, US, Asia excluding Japan, and Japan).

The 50% invested outside the UK is ***Dynamic Diversification*** in action, which I explored in chapter 19 in the context of *The Japan Problem.* So, if one area goes into seemingly terminal decline (as with Japan from 1989), you will be dynamically switched out.

Here is a table showing the performance and your extra growth. Although the extra is less than with the UK-only portfolio, you have the comfort of knowing you are somewhat better diversified.

Table 2: *50/50 Dynamic Portfolio* (2000-2016)

	Total Return	Extra growth on £100,000 investment
Dynamic Portfolio	329.46%	**£228,750 EXTRA GROWTH**
UK All Companies Sector Average	100.71%	
FTSE 100	85.43%	

The third category of investor likes a spread of funds across a variety of different assets, so is a tad more cautious. There might be some investment into stock market-linked funds, but also significant amounts (40%+) in other assets such as property and bond funds.

Unlike the first two categories, these investors are often not DIY investors, rather advised clients of the FundExpert parent, Dennehy Weller & Co. Because they are cautious, they are more inclined to seek professional, personalised advice.

At any one time, there might be up to 15 funds from 6-8 different fund sectors.

There are many permutations here to suit each taste, which could become another book on its own! For now, the performance in the next category gives you a taste of the success you can enjoy.

The last category would be similarly cautious to the latter, but this investor is content with a simpler solution. This might entail just three funds, where each fund holds a mixture of assets, including stock markets, bonds, and property. These are typically called multi-asset funds, for example the Mixed funds I highlighted on page 142.

For many of you reading this book, this person might sound dull, and you might think the results are equally uninspiring. You will be surprised, providing you do it properly.

In the table below, you can see the extra growth by using ***Dynamic Fund Ratings*** to choose the best fund from the Mixed 20-60% Shares fund sector – what used to be called the Cautious sector.

Not only does this technique hugely outperform the average growth of this sector, but over this period also provided more than twice as much growth as an index tracker, with almost half the level of volatility (the latter not shown in the table).

Table 3: *Cautious Dynamic Portfolio* (2000-2016)

	Total Return	Extra growth on £100,000 investment
Dynamic Portfolio	284.95%	**£192,340 EXTRA GROWTH**
Mixed 20-60% Sector Avg.	92.61%	
FTSE 100	85.43%	

Well, that's three very compelling examples of ***Dynamic Fund Ratings*** in action for four very typical clients – that couldn't be clearer or simpler.

There are a number of other portfolios, all equally impressive, which we monitor and update monthly via FundExpert.

For our example, great attention is given to our ***Bonkers Portfolio*** – it is what it says on the tin, but the track record is sky high, generating nearly 1,000% of growth from January 2000 to end 2016.

Use of these ratings enables you to create a wide range of highly profitable portfolios – there is something to meet all tastes.

NEXT STEPS

A simple but vital lesson from a master of this art. Plus a bonus from no less than Einstein.

23. What George Soros Taught Me

Another hero in our story is George Soros.

George Soros is one of the world's most famous and successful investors and worth $24bn – when he talks you should listen. What he highlighted was so basic as to be insulting – but most people who buy funds do NOT do this.

He said that as an experiment he:

> *"kept a diary in which I recorded the thoughts that went into my investment decisions... it was a roaring success, my fund never did better. It also produced a surprising result: I came out of the experiment with quite different expectations about the future."*[57]

This is quite an admission for such an extraordinary man.

Writing down why he made a decision meant he learnt from bad decisions. And he became much more confident about his future decisions – because they were based on clear, written reasons.

Remember what Albert Einstein said: you cannot solve a problem by continuing with the same thinking that created it.

If you don't write down why you made a decision, and it subsequently goes wrong, you can't begin to learn from this mistake.

I have already illustrated the extraordinary difference between success and mediocrity – **a key part of your future success might be no more than a pen and paper**.

By the way, you might be inclined to type your reasons into a laptop or tablet or some other electronic equivalent. I believe the physical writing down, in your own hand, is a more powerful technique – it is a more physical pre-commitment.

At this point, go back to chapter 8 where I posed the question: "how do you choose funds now?" and asked you to write down your answer on the blank page. I wanted you to be honest. If you haven't done it yet, do please go back and do it now, I'll give you a few minutes. Please be honest – it doesn't have to be an essay, perhaps just write down a few key words.

How's that? Done?

You probably didn't write down your reasons when you bought your funds, but if you had written down some key words might they have been:

- Low charges
- Like the fund manager
- Like top 10 holdings
- Good advert
- Compelling mailer
- Adviser recommendation
- Newspaper mention
- Friend mentioned it

And what information did you gather, and perhaps file away if not write down?

- Charges
- Top 10 holdings
- Fund manager tenure
- Size of fund
- Performance table
- Fund manager commentary
- Annual or six-month fund manager report
- Fund performance graph
- Age of the fund manager

Writing down what you did, and why you did it, is not just to try and encourage clear-thinking before you choose a fund. It also gives you a reference point. If something goes wrong, you can go back to what you wrote down. This enables you to learn – if it is clear that there was a flaw in your thinking, if you made a mistake, you can more easily learn from it if you wrote down your reasons at the time you invested.

Honestly, would any of the above reasons have been crucial to your likely success? This requires a lot of honesty and some self-criticism.

Did any of the information you gathered tell you anything about the likelihood of the future success of your fund choice?

I was at the end of the phone on one BBC radio Money Box Live show when a gentleman rang in and was very concerned that he couldn't easily get detailed information on the holdings within a fund. In some cases, he even found it difficult finding the top 10 holdings of a fund – he said that it was crucial to his decision-making to have at least details of the top 10 holdings.

Call me old-fashioned, but if someone has been good enough to ring the show, and the BBC have been kind enough to invite me on, I can't see any point in not giving a clear and honest reply (as politely as possible of course).

I mentioned a few sources where he should be able to get fund fact sheets showing top 10 holdings, and in some cases even give you access to 6- or 12-month reports listing all holdings.

But I also had to make clear that it was highly unlikely this would help him identify funds with outstanding potential.

As politely as possible, I pointed out that if he was able to judge whether a fund was good based on the shares it held (whether the top 10 or every single holding), he either could work as a fund manager or simply buy the individual shares himself and sidestep the fund.

Guess what? He was a bit put out and suggested I hadn't been very helpful. And there was a little uncomfortable shuffling on the seats in the studio too.

No one can accuse me of not being straightforward. I will not be unkind when someone is trying to find their way through what appears to them to be a minefield, but I will do them a disservice if I am less than honest.

Bottom line. Write down why you are buying a fund. Regularly review this reason, certainly at least 6 monthly. *Be honest with yourself* and think about whether this reason (or each of various reasons) had any real relevance as to:

- Whether you should have bought that fund in the first place.
- How the fund subsequently performed.

If you really want to take a big leap forward in the potential of your investing, you must be honest with yourself – you almost certainly will have to change one or two things you are doing now which you think are important. Otherwise you are falling into the trap identified by Einstein – you cannot solve a problem with the same thinking that created it.

NEXT STEPS

Let's build your plan to transform the potential of your fund choices.

24. Start This Plan Now

If you use an adviser, I hope this book will enable you to engage more positively with him or her – a good adviser will not have a problem with that. In appendix 1 is a list of questions you might pose.

For the rest of you (probably DIY investors, making your own investment decisions), I want you to start this plan now, while the ideas and solutions in this book are fresh in your mind.

If I am going to give you a blueprint, where should it begin?

Should it start with an easy win? Write your name and the date at the top of the paper!

Only kidding.

Perhaps you could start with stating your objective in simple terms: e.g. income or growth. Or your period for investment? Or your attitude to risk?

If some people honestly wrote down their plan, it might read:

> "I had ten grand to put in an ISA, and someone at work/my uncle/the newspaper/a bloke in the pub said have a punt on Mongolian Smaller Companies."

This isn't me being unkind. I have been told this sort of thing regularly by DIY investors – sometimes it's £10,000, often it's hundreds of thousands, sometimes investors with multi-million pound portfolios. Then after a moment of enlightenment, typically brought on by a thumping loss for which they were totally unprepared, they realise they must be able to do much better, but aren't yet sure how.

So where should this plan begin?

You must begin with the single thing which will have the biggest impact on your success.

It's not fund charges.

It's not knowing the top 10 holdings of a fund.

It's not knowing the fund manager's view on the markets.

Nor is it knowing how long they have managed their fund.

It is process. The one thing which has the biggest impact, by far, on your success is whether you have a method, a process, to identify a fund or funds with outstanding potential. You have now seen a volume of compelling evidence showing you how a proven process can transform your success as an investor.

Now we are going to build your personal ***Winning Funds Blueprint.*** This is the foundation of reports for advisory clients which normally cost at least £500 – but for you it is a free resource included with this book.

BONUS DOWNLOAD

Your blueprint steps are all set out below. But for your convenience you can also download this at ***FundExpert.co.uk/blueprint***, and scribble to your hearts content, remembering what we learnt from George Soros in the last chapter.

The downloaded version also has additional notes and is updated based on feedback of other readers just like you.

Step 1: What is your preferred method for selecting funds?

There is certainly more than one way to select funds, but I believe there are very few which can pass the test represented by the checklist at the end of this section.

In this book, I have concentrated on one, ***Dynamic Fund Ratings***, and have shown you in great detail how this method could transform your success with funds.

So, the first question is straightforward.

Which method will you use to select funds?

- ☐ Dynamic Fund Ratings

Or

- ☐ A.N. Other

Tick one of the above boxes.

If you are still inclined to consider A.N. Other rating method, all I ask is that you honestly judge it against the checklist below, otherwise you have wasted your time reading this book.

CHECKLIST

What does a winning rating system look like?

Are you considering another rating method? That's no problem. But it MUST have these characteristics or it is not worthy of your time, your effort, and your money:

- It must be straightforward to identify **outstanding** funds
- The underlying **process** must be clear and understandable
- It must be **repeatable**
- There must be solid **evidence**, over a long period, illustrating how these ratings have generated extra growth

If you have an adviser ask them to explain their basis for selecting funds.

Step 2: Who will be your "buddy"?

An effective process to identify funds with outstanding potential is ***the*** essential foundation of your success – that is why it was the first step of this plan, your plan.

But one big problem remains – YOU. I'll keep saying this. You are the biggest reason why this plan will fail. Believe me we all share this problem – but there is a solution.

It's all about discipline. Are you so well-organised that you will undertake your 6 monthly review? Always? For years to come? And will you review your funds when the market is in a tizzy? Or will you just put your head in the sand and pretend it's not happening?

It isn't because you inherently lack discipline. More often, it is as simple as interventions by life and its many distractions. This is coupled with some inconvenient and hard-wired bad habits, particularly when faced with uncertainty (see chapter 9).

If this is to work, if you are going to stay focussed, **you need a buddy**.

Someone who will nudge you into action at the right times.

Every 6 months. Year after year. Without fail.

A buddy is essential to your success, and it is what we have now created at **FundExpert.co.uk/buddy**. It involves you in little effort, a lot less stress – and can transform your investing results.

Tick one box below to identify who will provide your "buddy" service, to keep you focussed and disciplined.

☐ FundExpert

Or

☐ A.N. Other

Make sure you check out how our buddy system will work for you – go to **www.FundExpert.co.uk/buddy**

Step 3: What level of volatility are you comfortable with?

If you can define a bit more accurately the market ups and downs with which you would be comfortable, this will identify the sorts of funds, the fund sectors, from which you will make your selections.

Answer the questions below as honestly as possible by ticking the box next to your answer.

Questions	Strongly Agree	Agree	Neither Disagree nor Agree	Disagree	Strongly Disagree
I try to make as much money as possible				✓	
My knowledge of financial terms is extensive	✓				
I like the excitement of investing in volatile foreign markets for higher returns		✓			
I am used to taking financial risk		✓			
Financial press is a major influence on my investment decisions					✓
	1	2	3	4	5
Totals	1	4		4	5

Now total up the number of ticks in each column and multiply this total by the number at the bottom of the column.

For example, if you ticked "disagree" 3 times, multiply this by the number at the bottom (4) and write this total at the bottom of the column – in this case 12 (being 3 x 4).

Do that for each column and then add the column totals together and write them here:

Your Total Risk Score: 14

Now write this number in the appropriate row below and you have an early indication of your investor type.

	What type of investor are you?	
Investor Type	**Risk Scores**	**Your total Risk Score**
1. – Very defensive	24-25	
2. – Cautious	18-23	
3. – Balanced	13-17	14
4. – Balanced with a sense of adventure	9-12	
5. – Aggressive	5-8	

Don't panic. If you have answered the questions as honestly as you can, your category in the above table is a decent starting point to take you forward. You can always review it later if you feel it is not a fair category for you.

Step 4: Do you prefer focussed funds or a simple solution?

- ☐ I prefer to buy only specialist or ***focussed funds*** (up to 15 funds)
- ☐ I prefer a ***simple solution*** with multi asset funds (up to 5 funds)

Tick one of the boxes above

NB If you answered "simple solution" above, the answer to the next step must be "mixed asset classes".

Step 5: What level of diversification would you like?

- ☐ I want exposure to just one focussed sector or asset class
e.g. UK stock market
- ☐ I want exposure to more than one asset class, and globally diversify
e.g. 50% UK stock market, 50% stock markets outside the UK
- ☑ I want exposure to a **mix of asset classes**, with different levels of volatility
e.g. stock markets, bonds, and property

Tick one of the boxes above

Step 6: How often do you want to actively review your funds?

This is a trick question really. If you opted for ***Dynamic Fund Ratings*** in Step 1, you should review every 6 months. This is just to reinforce that point.

- ☑ Every 6 months
- ☐ A.N. Other

Tick one of the boxes above

Step 7: Let's identify your fund sectors

You now know how you will identify funds with outstanding potential, probably using ***Dynamic Fund Ratings***.

You also know:

- Who will be your investment "buddy" to keep you on the straight-and-narrow.
- The level of day-to-day volatility with which you are comfortable (your Investor Type, step 3).
- Your preferred diversification or spread of investments types.
- Whether you prefer to use a large number of specialist funds or a small number of mixed funds.
- How often you will review (probably every 6 months).

Now you need to identify the fund sectors from which you will identify your winning funds.

To do this, if you haven't already, you must download your blueprint from FundExpert.co.uk/blueprint.

BONUS – FUND SECTOR MATRIX

At the time of writing, the ***Winning Funds Blueprint*** also includes our ***Fund Sector Matrix***. This enables you to quickly identify the sectors from which you must select your funds based on all of your answers above.

Go to **FundExpert.co.uk/blueprint**

Let's recap – what have you achieved?

You have now built a plan which is the foundation of your investing success from today onwards, for years to come. This is so whether you are a novice or a very experienced investor.

If you are already quite experienced, you probably had a niggly naggly feeling that you could do much better. If you are a relative novice, the personalised blueprint you have just created means you have already leap-frogged what many advisers could have offered you.

One Thing Missing

You have come a long way, and you now know the fund sectors from which you should choose your winning funds, just as Harry did in chapter 11.

If you are experienced, and have the time, you can probably go to your usual source of fund information (as Harry did) and you are on your way to identify those funds.

If you haven't the time, or are a novice, we make this easy for you.

One Small Step

If you would like us to make it easy for you to quickly identify those winning funds, to put everything you have just learnt and built into practice, there is only one small step left...

25. One Small Step

I hope you have enjoyed your journey through this book. From the history explaining how we got to the point where too many funds fail; to the towering examples of success, and how these are within your reach right now.

And lastly the ***Winning Funds Blueprint***, which is at the heart of a report for advisory clients that would cost a minimum of £500 – but you got it for free!

Obviously, I could not provide detail here on individual funds as this is continually changing. But I am determined that you should have access to ***winning funds right now***, so I have made these available in the easiest possible form, in one document, which we update every month for new readers. Here's the detail:

LATEST WINNING FUNDS, SECTOR BY SECTOR

Go to FundExpert.co.uk/latestwinningfunds

LET'S FINISH THE JOB

This fund list, in this straightforward format, is not even available to paying subscribers! It doesn't stop there:

- **Your own "Winning Funds Blueprint".** You should already have downloaded this.
- **Worked examples** to guide your next steps.
- **Your burning questions?** I will answer them in my regular live teleconference.
- **Top-performing model portfolios**, including weekly performance updates.
- **LATEST** winning funds report, sector by sector, to finish off your blueprint or plan.
- The latest edition of the acclaimed **TopFunds Guide**, usual cost £50.
- **Our historical research**.
- **BONUS** - My ebook histories "**The 1987 Crash**" and "**The Technology Bubble**".
- **PLUS** You will discover how unique smart technology will keep you on the straight and narrow for years to come.

There are a number of other resources for you, with my compliments. I will be adding to this list all the time.

The cost? Oh yes I forgot.

How would you feel if all of this was free? That would be bonkers wouldn't it?

And thank you for coming this far with me. I hope you have enjoyed it as much as I have.

LATEST WINNING FUNDS, SECTOR BY SECTOR

Go to FundExpert.co.uk/latestwinningfunds

LET'S FINISH THE JOB

Appendix 1
Questions for advisers and their clients

If you intend using an adviser, you now have a decent level of knowledge to ask them a few questions – and don't be afraid to put these in writing and ask for a written reply – that should be no bother for a decent adviser who is serious about doing the best for you:

- Do you/your firm construct my portfolio and choose my funds?
- How do you construct my portfolio? Do you have an in-house process, or do you rely on a third party, in particular third party software?
- How do you choose my funds? Does this process meet these 4 criteria... (see chapter 24, Step 1)
- How often do you review the funds?
- What is the basis for the review? e.g. for what reason would you replace a fund?

- If you do none of the above, and contract this out to a discretionary management service, can they answer all the above questions?
- Whether you or a third party build my portfolio and select funds, can you provide a track record over at least the last 5 years versus the UK stock market and deposit?

If you are an adviser, and wish to adopt the approach in this book for your clients, please contact **Sam.Lees@fundexpert.co.uk.**

Endnotes

1. *Vintage Funds Report 2014*

2. *Vintage Funds Report 2014*

3. *01/07/1994 - 30/06/2014. Simple proven process in the style of Harry's portfolio (chapter 11).*

4. *Vintage Funds Report 2014*

5. *"The Origins of Mutual Funds", K. Geert Rouwenhorst, Yale School of Management, March 2003*

6. *"Unit Trusts from The Beginning", Christopher Hill, 1984*

7. *"Capital Ideas", Peter Bernstein, 20015 (p142)*

8. *31/12/1970 - 31/12/1974, FTSE All Share index (GBP, price-only)*

9. *29/12/1999 - 12/03/2003, FTSE 100 index (GBP, price-only)*

10. *"Against The Gods", Peter Bernstein, P135 onwards. This is a must read if you would like more in-depth analysis, beautifully written.*

11. *Barclays Equity Gilt Study, 2015. Dividends and interest re-invested*

12. *"Against The Gods", Peter Bernstein, P248 onwards*

13. *By Charles Mackay, first published in 1841. Sometimes called the best book ever written about market psychology*

14. *First published in 1978, latest edition December 2000, a history of the nature of financial crises.*

15. *"Triumph of the Optimists", Dimson, Marsh, Staunton, 2002*

16. *Ian Stewart, Emeritus Professor of Mathematics, University of Warwick, and author of "17 Equations That Changed The World"*

17. *"The Big Short", Michael Lewis, 2010*

18. *"The (Mis)Behaviour of Markets" Benoit Mandelbrot. First published 2004.*

19. *Fundexpert.co.uk*

20. *"Global Investment Returns Yearbook", Dimson, Marsh and Staunton – London Business School*

21. *1955-2015, Numis Smaller Companies Index vs FTSE All Share, 1955-2015.*

22. *Fundexpert.co.uk/highyieldresearch*

23. *Fundexpert.co.uk/incomeinvesting*

24. *Value" being based on price-to-book, second decile. See "What Works on Wall Street", O'Shaugnessy, 1996, pages 170-171*

25. *"Behavioural Investing", James Montier, first edition 2007*

26. *"Thinking Fast and Slow", Daniel Kahneman, first published 2011*

27. "Action bias among elite soccer goalkeepers", Michael Bar-Elia, Ofer H. Azara, and others: Journal of Economic Psychology, January 2007.

28. *"Prospect Theory", Kahneman and Tversky, 1979*

29. *Precisely why our old brain developed this tendency is open to debate. But it is interesting that psychologist Laurie Santos even observed this behaviour in Capuchin monkeys*

30. *"The disposition effect and under-reaction to news", Andrea Frazzini, 2006*

31. *"Are investors reluctant to realize their losses?", Terrance Odean, 1998*

32. *"The Little Book of Behavioural Investing" James Montier, first edition 2010*

33. *Within the term "flight" I would also include that I call The Ostrich Effect – when you are faced with uncertainty or a threat there is often a tendency to pretend it isn't happening, as if by*

ignoring it it will go away. Inertia generally is a terrible problem for investors.

34. *Dalbar Report 2015, produced yearly.*

35. *FTSE 100 (GBP, total return) 6/10/1997 to 12/11/1997.*

36. *FTSE 100: 29/12/1999 - 12/03/2003. "Harry's portfolio": +134.22% (1/7/1994 - 12/3/2003). GBP, total return.*

37. *FTSE 100: 12/03/2003 - 24/05/2007. "Harry's portfolio": +206.22% (12/3/2003 - 24/05/2007). GBP, total return.*

38. *FTSE 100 (GBP, total return).*

39. *01/07/1994 - 09/03/2009. Index tracker = Aviva Inv UK Index Tracking fund (+71.27%). GBP, total return.*

40. *Fundexpert.co.uk/DynamicFundSelection*

41. *Fundexpert.co.uk/MomentumResearch*

42. *Alfred Cowles and Herbert Jones, 1937*

43. "Margin of Safety", Seth Klarman, first published in 1991

44. *5-year period: 3/1/2011 - 31/12/2015, price-only. Berkshire Hathaway = Adjusted Close price of BRK-B shares. Dynamic Fund Portfolio = top 3 funds from UK All Companies sector on a 6-month review. Indices: S&P 500 (price-only, USD); FTSE All Share (price-only, GBP).*

45. *31/01/1995 - 05/03/2014. Invesco Perpetual Income fund. GBP, total return.*

46. *Fundexpert.co.uk/MomentumResearch*

47. *1/7/1994 - 31/12/2015. Dynamic Fund Portfolio = top 3 funds from UK All Companies sector on a 6-month review. GBP, total return.*

48. *Some people will use other definitions.*

49. "Fooled by Randomness", first published in 2002

50. *Nikkei 225: 1/1/1990 - 31/12/2016, JPY, price-only.*

51. *31/12/2010 - 31/12/2015. Sector averages of Sterling Corporate Bond and UK All Companies,* GBP, total return.

52. *31/12/2010 - 31/12/2015.*

53. *Fund B/X: Franklin UK Mid Cap. Fund C/Y: HSBC FTSE All Share Index. 31/12/2005 to 31/12/2015, GBP, total return.*

54. *01/07/1994 - 30/06/2014. Average fund = UK All Companies sector average, GBP, total return.*

55. I have not mentioned taxes, which might also impact on your choices, but are beyond the scope of this book. In addition I have not mentioned your time horizon for investment, which should be at least 10 years.

56. This book is dedicated to investors whose objective is growth. If your objective is to generate income we have some great resources on FundExpert.co.uk, including a unique tool to help you identify the income funds which suit you best.

57. "Alchemy of finance", George Soros, first published 1987

INDEX

SYMBOLS

A

B

C

D

E

F

G

33895016R00125

Printed in Great Britain
by Amazon